JAINA PENANCE

JAINA PENANCE

CHAMPAT RAI JAIN

GYAN

Published by

Gyan Publishing House
5, Ansari Road
Daryaganj, New Delhi-110002
Phone: 011-47034999, 9811692060
E-mail: books@gyanbooks.com

Distribution Network
gyanbooks.com
India, USA, Canada, UK, Australia

ISBN: 978-93-7447-456-3 (PB)

First Published, 1930

2nd Impression 2025

Printed at: Gyan Press, Delhi.

JAINA PENANCE
Author: CHAMPAT RAI JAIN

JAINA PENANCE

JAINA PENANCE

BY

CHAMPAT RAI JAIN

VIDYAVARIDHI, BARRISTER-AT-LAW

ALLAHABAD:

THE INDIAN PRESS, LTD.

1930

PREFACE

The 'Jaina Penance' deals with the rules laid down in the Jaina Religion for the purification of different kinds of individuals, who wish to follow the Path of the Great Conquerors (JINAS). It is based on the authority of the "Prāyaśchitta Samuchchaya," the authorship of which is ascribed to Saint Gurudasji, a Jaina *āchārya* (Leader of Saints) of the Digambara sect.

The author's age is not known; in fact no Digambara Saint is known to have borne that name. Perhaps he only describes himself as *guru-das* (the attendant or slave of his preceptor)! There is an ancient commentary on the work which was composed by Śri Nandi Guru. But who this saint was is not known. According to Mr. Nathu Ram Premi (see the preface to the Prāyaśchitta Sangraha), he might have been the Preceptor (*guru*) of Saint Śri Chandra who composed his "Purāṇasāra" in 1070 *Samvat* Era (=1014 A.D.). He was called Śri Nandi. He would thus be living in the 10th century A.D. There was another Śri Nandi Saint. His pupil was Nayanandi whose pupil Nemichandra was the preceptor of Saint Basunandi who is known to have lived in the 12th century of the *Samvat* Era. Probably the preceptor of Saint Śri Chandra and of Śri Nayanandi was the one and the same Śri Nandi. If these conclusions be correct then the commentary referred to would be deemed to have been composed in the 10th century A.D., so that the original work must be at least about a thousand years old.

The book has been translated into Hindi by Sjt. Panna Lalji Soni, who was at one time the chief Pandit of the Gopal Siddhānta Vidyālaya, Morena (Gwalior State). The present work is chiefly based on this Hindi translation. I am, however, giving the Sanskrit text in Part III.

The original work is composed in poetry which seems to have been much in vogue at the time of its composition, and which is, no doubt, responsible for the lack of precision which is found to obscure the interpretation of some of the *ślokas* (couplets). The Hindi translation is not critical. However, the number of the verses that actually resist elucidation is very very small. An endeavour has been made here to get at the true teaching underlying the various obscure texts, and I have consulted several saints and learned men on the subject to ascertain the true reading.

It has, however, not been found necessary to enter into an elaborate discussion of these obscure points; I am merely content to give what seems to me to be the true interpretation of the various texts. A part of the aforesaid element of confusion has, no doubt, also arisen from the jumbling together of the diverse texts in an indiscriminate manner, which might be due to careless copying or some other similar cause.

The "Prāyaśchitta Samuchchaya" consists of two

parts, the book proper and a *chūlikā* or supplement. The verses of the two parts are separately numbered in the original. In the references I have adhered to the numbering of the author, and indicated the book proper by merely its *śloka* number (thus Ś. 101, Ś 159, etc.), and the Chūlikā by the abbreviation Ch. (thus Ch. 101, Ch. 159 and so forth).

A knowledge of the rules applicable to the householder and the saint is presupposed in the reader if he will appreciate the merit of the penances prescribed and of the fine distinctions on which they are grounded. Brief explanatory notes have been given in some places to elucidate difficult and obscure points, but it is not possible to incorporate the whole of the Jaina *Charitra* Code (rules relating to disciplinary conduct) in the present work.

In the Appendix I have given the penances provided for the householders' transgressions in the "Prāyaśchitta Grantha" which is included in the "Prāyaśchitta Sangraha," published by the Manickchand Digambara Jaina Grantha Mālā Samiti of Bombay. This book professes to be from the pen of the great Bhattākalankadeva whose name is a household word in the Jaina community. But, as the learned secretary of the M.D.J.G. Samiti observes, it does not appeal to one's mind as an authoritative work, and certainly it could not have been composed by such a profound Jaina scholar as Akalankadeva whose authority it seeks to claim for itself. Its composition would seem to have been influenced by the spirit of the latter-day commercialized Hinduism, as is evident from such penances as the gift of kine, flowers, betel-leaves and gold, which are quite opposed to the teaching of Jainism.

As for the two other books on the subject, namely, the "Chheda Pinda" and the "Chheda Śāstra" which are included in the "Prāyaśchitta Sangraha" already referred to, help has been taken from them in the compilation of the work on which this treatise is grounded, and no further reference to them seems necessary or called for under the circumstances.

JAINA HOSTEL:
ALLAHABAD.
6th November, 1929.

C. R. JAIN.

CONTENTS

PART III

CHAPTER I

GENERAL OBSERVATIONS

Prāyaśchitta is the cause of the destruction of the evil effect of *karmas*. All serious-minded aspirants are ever eager to preserve the purity of the mind undefiled, and at once resort to measures to remove the taint, if a blemish is noticed by them in their conduct, that is, thought, word or deed.

Prāyaśchitta is very pleasing to the generality of men, especially to the community of the pious householders (laity). Disciplinary vows are useless in the absence of the rectifying penance; and no conduct can be deemed bright or purposeful whose faults are not noted nor corrected. In short, without penance there can be no proper conduct; without proper conduct there can be no *dharma* (religion or piety); and without *dharma* salvation cannot be attained.[1]

The word *prāyaśchitta* is derived from *prāyo*, the people or pious folk, and *chitta*, mind: hence what is pleasing to the mind of the pious folk is

[1] Ś. 5.

prāyaśchitta. It may also be derived from *prāyao, tapaścharaṇa* (asceticism), and *chitta*, establishing; hence it means the establishing of the mind properly in the observance of the rules relating to austerities. According to another derivation, it comes from *prāya*, the community of saints, and *chitta*, that which attracts the heart, and signifies the action that is pleasing to the heart of a saint. *Prāya* also signifies a fault, and *chitta* is its atonement or eradication. Thus, *prāyaśchitta* is intended for the purification of the soul and for the eradication of the taint of evil from the heart.[1]

Confession is enjoined on all people who have embarked on the voyage of self-conquest by means of disciplinary vows. It has been said that one should not conceal one's faults from a doctor, a preceptor and a benevolent king.[2]

Prāyaśchitta has two aspects, the spiritual or higher (*niśchaya*) and the physical or lower (*vyavahāra*). The *niśchaya* is the *prāyaśchitta* proper in reality. It consists in washing away the taint of evil by self-contemplation, that is to say, by immersion in the true Self, so to speak! All shortcomings are washed away speedily, that way, by the ablutions with the purifying 'Vision of the Self.' The

[1] Ś.182. [2] Ch. 162.

longing to wash away the stain is itself, in reality, the greatest penance.[1] Confession itself is half the amends.[2] What is really meant is a heartfelt regret for the deed, which implies a determination not to do it again in the future. Unless the regret and the determination to refrain from the sinful act are present in the mind, confession will not be of much help. It should be noted that the saint endowed with the Right Faith will not be content till he succeeds in eradicating the very source of evil action from his heart, since he knows and fears the consequences of the evil path and the loss of *dharma*.[3]

Thus confession itself is the *vyavahāra* penance, and the symbol of the presence of the *niśchaya* regret. If it is omitted deliberately, that means that the saint is still averse to 'lowering' himself that way, which is consistent only with the presence and activity of the element of pride, itself a bad and undesirable trait in the saintly character. As a matter of fact, only those men are considered great who cheerfully long to perform expiation for their shortcomings.[4] They excel as leaders and attain to heavens and ultimately also to *nirvāna*.

Thus, the *niśchaya* and the *vyavahāra* forms of penances go together, hand in hand. The type of

[1] Ch. 160. [2] Ch. 159. [3] Ch. 157. [4] Ch. 164.

the former determines the amount of the latter. Where it is present in abundance, the latter will only be nominally enforced; otherwise *chheda* (de-gradation), *mūla* (re-ordination) and *parihāra* (expulsion) even may have to be resorted to, in severe cases of breach of discipline.

All kinds of penances are to be freely used, subject to the conditions of time, place, individual capacity and the like.[1] For the first fault, however, it is not usual to give the extreme penalty, though there may be cases that demand even this kind of treatment, *e.g.*, the ravishing of the wife of one's king, or engineering a revolution. But no hard and fast rules can be laid down which will govern all cases. Discretion must be employed in meting out punishment to the delinquents in every case,[2] and the proper penance should be determined carefully, with due regard to the conditions and circumstances attending the transgression.[3] Above all it should not be forgotten that the object is not punishment but reclamation, and the safeguarding of the interests of the sinner and the community of the saints.

As a general rule, a strong man should be given any form of penance; he who is nervous or easily upset should be given that form of penance only which is

[1] Ch. 161. [2] Ś. 128. [3] Ś.148.

calculated to help him in ridding himself of his lack of composure. Weakly persons should be given what is helpful in regaining strength or at least what will not constitute a drain on their already poor store of energy; those who are deficient both in regard to physical strength and mental composure should be treated even more lightly than the above.[1]

No one is immune from penance—not even the highest saintly dignitary, nor the *āchārya* (Leader of saints) himself. But their faults (confessions) are not to be published to the world.[2] Where the Leader has himself been guilty of a fault he should undergo the penance secretly if his evil action was not noticed by any one; otherwise publicly, as in the case of the ordinary saints.[3]

If the *āchārya* is himself required to undergo penitential expiation he should convene a conference of his *sangha*, and instruct them as to the rules applicable to his case and invite them to determine the amount of the penance for him, or he may determine the penalty himself, if the *sangha* be untrained.

It is not possible to frame a handy code of penances that will actually cover every case. The general rules, if applied discriminately, will, however, be found to meet all cases that arise in the lives of the truly pious people, and would present sufficient

[1] Ś. 148. [2] Ch. 125. [3] Ch. 111.

guidance for all emergencies. Guidance may also be taken from the penances prescribed for similar breaches of the saintly 'etiquette.'[1] To be absolutely just one will have to notice all the various shades of sinful mentality whose number is legion.[2] No one can be expected to emerge successfully from a quest for the right penance for every shade and grade of the sinner, under the circumstances. It is, therefore, very very essential that the Leader should be a practical man, who does not delight in needless hair-splitting but who is able to handle a situation in a judicious and practical manner, there and then.

The Leader-*āchārya* is alone qualified to prescribe the proper penance. No one else in the *sangha* (community of saints) should usurp that function. The *āchārya* himself should be a well-trained person, and one who is endowed with great wisdom and experience and the knowledge of the actual conditions of existence in the land. He should have a well-controlled nature, and should be possessed of a capacity for the judicial function that he is required to exercise, in regard to the transgressions by his disciples and followers. No one who is not so endowed is qualified to hear confessions or to apportion the penance.[3]

[1] Ch. 158. [2] Ch. 163. [3] Ś. 183.

CHAPTER II

TYPES OF PENANCE

Expiatory penances are of ten kinds as follows:—

(1) *Ālochanā* (confession);

(2) *Pratikramaṇa* (blaming oneself for the fault committed);

(3) *Tadubhaya* (*ālochanā+pratikramaṇa* combined);

(4) *Viveka* or *tyāga* (giving up or refraining from the use of certain articles of food, if they tend to excite passions, or are suspected to be impure, or are eaten in forgetfulness of a previous vow or resolve to avoid them);

(5) *Vyutsarga* (performing *kāyotsarga* for a fixed period, and remaining unmoving in one posture all the time);

(6) *Tapa* (fasting or imposing restrictions on the taking of food);

(7) *Chheda* (degrading);

(8) *Mūla* (re-ordination, *i.e.*, complete loss of rank);

(9) *Parihāra* also termed *anupasthāna*, *anupasthāpanā* and *pinchha* (humiliating, or expulsion, for a time, from the *sangha i.e.*, community);

(10) *Śraddhāna* (re-admission into the faith).

The above are all the recognized forms of penance. In addition to them there is another kind of penance which is known as *vaiyāvṛitya* (service or nursing). This is comprised in the *parihāra* penance, according to strict classification. The form known as *pāranchika* signifies expulsion, full and complete, and is but another word for *parihāra*. *Parihāra* is termed *pinchha* because of the person who is undergoing it being required to hold his feather whisk (the *pichhi*) in front of him, as a mark whereby it may be known that he is undergoing that form of penance.

Bathing is recommended in case of contact with an unclean person, *e. g.*, a *pariah.*[1] Elsewhere one *kāyotsarga* is provided as the proper penalty for such a contact.[2] Bathing is said to be of three kinds: with water, with the holy *mantras* (recitation) and with disciplinary vows.[3]

[1] Ch. 136. [2] Ś. 29. [3] Ch. 136.

CHAPTER III

EXPLANATION OF CERTAIN TECHNICALITIES

Āchāmla = the taking of food consisting only of one kind of grain with water, and includes rice-water, with or without grains of rice soaked in it.

Ekasthāna = means either (1) eating only from one dish, pot or pan, and only as much as has been taken out at one time, whether it be only a tea-spoonful or more, in the case of pulses, vegetables and the like, and only one *roti*, or puri, etc., in the case of more substantial things, or (2) going without food or discontinuing the process of eating, if one has to shift one's position from any cause. If the position has to be shifted before the releasing of what is termed *veerya mudrā* there is no harm ; but afterwards food is forbidden even though eating has not commenced as yet.

Note.—A saint places his right hand on his right shoulder when starting for his food. The position is called *veerya mudrā*. It is released only when the saint has made up his mind to accept the food, and after he is satisfied that it is unobjectionable in every way. He is free to shift his position if the one he has taken up is, or becomes, unsuitable from any cause; but not after he has released the *mudrā*. If the necessity for shifting arise subsequent to the act of release he must go without food at the time altogether, though not one morsel has been taken by him.

Nirvikṛiti = unsavoury, that is, *rasa*-less food. The *rasas* are: milk, curd, *ghee*, oil, sugar and salt.

Upavāsa = a fast.

Purumandala = refraining from food till after the mid-day *sāmāyika* (*i.e.*, 1-15 p.m.)

Kalyānaka = one each of the quintette of *āchāmla*, *nirvikṛiti*, *purumandala*, *ekasthāna* and *upavāsa*.

4 *Kalyānakas* = 1 *bhinnamāsa*.

5 *Kalyānakas* = 1 *gurumāsa*.

5 *Kalyānakas* *minus* the *nirvikṛitis*, *āchāmlas*, or *upavāsas* = 1 *laghumāsa*. According to the Chheda Śāstra, a *laghumāsa* consists of 5 *upavāsas* and 5 each of three other items out of the remaining four. A *Laghumāsa* also signifies the observance of the *pancha-kalyānaka* with regular intervals.

5 *Kalyānakas* = *svasthāna* = *māsika* = *mūla guṇa* = *mūla* and *gurūmāsa*. A *Pancha kalyānaka* is the continuous observance without interruption of a *kalyānaka* five times.

Ṣaṣṭha = 1 two-days' fast with only one meal each on the day preceding the commencement and the day following the observance.

Kshamaṇa = *upavāsa*.

Chāturamāsa = 4 *pancha kalyānakas*, or continuous fasting, on alternate days, for four months.

Mithyākāra = (literally, it may be annulled), a form of regret; dissociation with the result of a sin committed by oneself; "may this action of mine be annulled!"

Nyama = daily self-examination for the faults committed. The evening *nyama* commences before the disk of the sun has half disappeared below the horizon, and the morning one should end before the dawn.

Locha = fasting, with regular intervals, for the period of a *locha*. Locha signifies plucking out the hair, which is recommended to be performed after every two, three or four months. In the case of a short *locha* (with a duration of two months) a meal is allowed after every three days' fast; in that of the middling one, a meal is allowed after every two days' fast, and in the case of the longer *locha* alternately with a fast.

Salutation *mantram* = णमो अर्हंताणं, णमो सिद्धाणं, णमो आइरियाणं, णमो उवज्झायणं, णमो लोये सव्व साहुणं ।

(Ṇamo Arhantāṇam, ṇamo Siddhāṇam, ṇamo Āiriyāṇam, ṇamo Uvajjhāyāṇam, ṇamo loye savva sāhuṇam). It means:

I salute the *Arhant*;
I salute the *Siddha*;
I salute the *Āchāryas* (Leaders of Saints);
I salute the *Upādhyāyas* (Teacher Saints);
I salute all *Sādhus* (holy Saints)!

1 *Kāyotsarga* = recitation of the holy Salutation *mantram* nine times, without shifting one's position, and keeping the mind, speech and the body under control.

1 Devasika Kāyotsarga	= 108	Salutation	*mantras.*
1 Pākshika	,,	= 300	,,	,,
1 Chaturmāsika	,,	= 400	,,	,,
1 Samvatsarika	,,	= 500	,,	,,

CHAPTER IV

VALUATIONS AND EQUATIONS

1	*Purumandal*	= $\frac{1}{4}$ of an *upavāsa* (fast)
1	*Nirvikṛiti*	= $\frac{1}{3}$ of an *upavāsa*.
1	*Ekasthāna*	= $\frac{1}{2}$ of an *upavāsa*, but it implies a greater degree of 'suffering' than *nirvikṛiti*.
1	*Āchāmla*	= $\frac{3}{4}$ of an *upavāsa*.
12	*Kāyotsargas*	= 1 *upavāsa*.
1	Fast	= 108 recitations of the great Salutation *mantram*.
1	„	= 200 recitations of the 16-lettered अर्हंत, सिद्ध, आयरिय, उवज्झाय, साहू (*Arhant*, *Siddha*, *Āyariya*, *Uvajjhāya*, *Sādhu*),
1	„	= 300 recitations of the 6-lettered अर्हंत सिसा (*Arhantsisā*).
1	„	= 400 recitations of the 4-lettered अर्हंत (*Arhant*).
1	„	= 500 recitations of the monosyllable ओम (*Aum*).
1	„	= 500 recitations of the vowel अ (*A*).

108 Recitations of the Salutation *mantram* = 1 *Devasika kāyotsarga* = 1 fast.

300 Recitations of the Salutation *mantram* = 1 *Pākshika kāyotsarga*.

400 Recitations of the Salutation *mantram* = 1 *Chaturmāsika kāyotsarga*.

500 Recitations of the Salutation *mantram* = 1 *Samvatsarika kāyotsarga*.

CHAPTER V

TYPES OF MEN

There are many types of men. They have been described as follows :—

1. the *śraddhāvāna* (devoted to religion),
2. the *aśraddhāvāna* (not devoted, that is, indifferent to religion),
3. the *mṛidu* (meek),
4. the *garvi* (proud), who is either proud of his rank, that is seniority, or of his austerities.
5. the *gitārtha* (endowed with much philosophical wisdom),
6. the *agitārtha* (not endowed with philosophical wisdom),
7. the *alpavita* or *alpaśruta* (having slight scriptural knowledge),
8. the *durbala* (who is physically weak),
9. the *nīchasanghatah* (endowed with an inferior system of bony formation),
10. the *sarvapurṇa* (endowed with one of the

higher types of bony formation and well-qualified otherwise, except for the lack of control of sleep),

11. the *ātmasmartha* (who does not wish for *vaiyāvṛitya* (service) but is not disturbed otherwise by the expiation prescribed),
12. the *ubhayatara* (who also wishes for the *vaiyāvṛitya*),
13. the *anyatara* (who voluntarily undertakes the other also when required to perform either *tapa* or *vaiyāvṛitya* alone),
14. the *anubhaya* (who is unable to perform either *vaiyāvṛitya* or *tapa*, and who has, therefore, to be given the milder forms of penance, *āchāmla* and like),
15. the *paratara* (who is greatly terrified with *tapa*, and who, therefore, prays for the *vaiyāvṛitya*),
16. the *āchārya* (leaders of saints themselves),
17. the *pradhāna* (other eminent saints),
18. the *bhikshu* (ordinary saints).

According to another classification, saints are divided into two classes, namely, the *sāpeksha* and the *nirpeksha*. The *sāpekshas* are those who expect compassion or kindness from their leader; the *nirpekshas* do not expect either. These may be further subdivided as follows :—

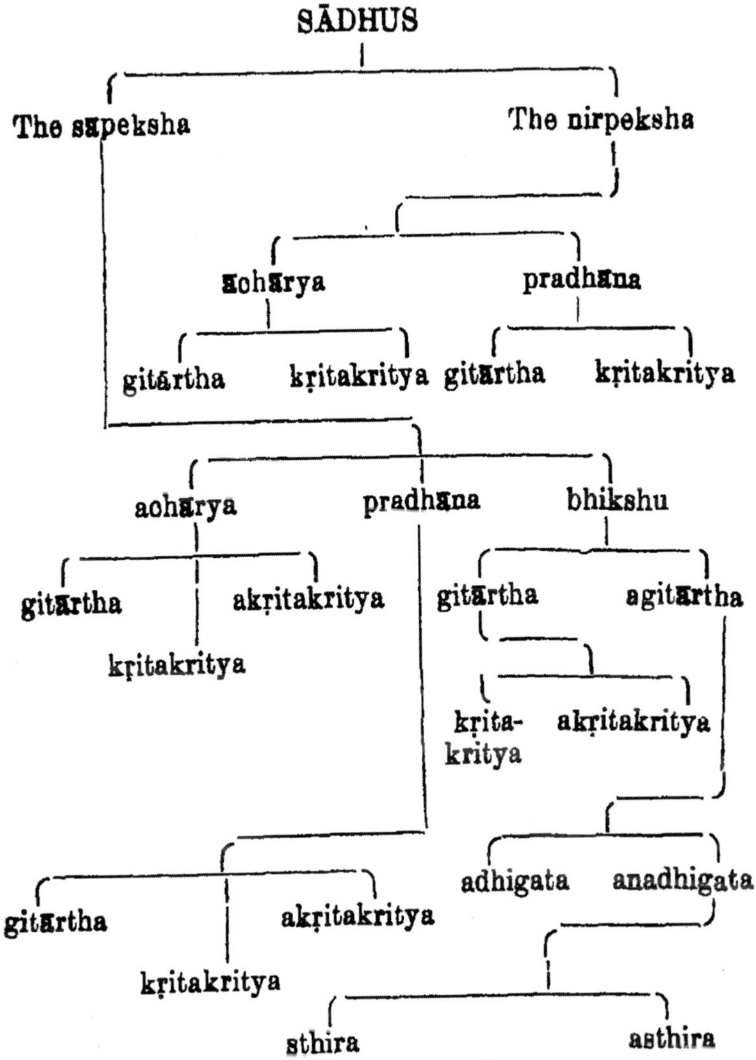

The explanation of the technical terms used here is as follows:—

The *gitārtha* = the illumined philosopher or the knower of the entirety of the scriptural wisdom.

The *agitārtha* = the unillumined; the unenlightened; he who is not endowed with philosophical insight.

The *kṛitakritya* = given to preaching.

The *akṛitakritya* = he who does not preach.

The *adhigata* = who is ignorant of the scriptural wisdom, but is able to think for himself.

The *anadhigata* = the unlearned and unthinking personage who only knows what he has heard from his preceptor.

The *sthira* = he who is firmly established in faith.

The *asthira* = who is unbalanced in respect of the rules of right conduct.

Men have also been divided into two rough divisions according as they observe the root or foundation principles (*mūla guṇas*) or are able to keep their elaborations (*uttara guṇas*) also. The former are called the *mūla-guṇa-dhāri* (observers of the root virtues) and the latter the *uttara-guṇa-dhāri*.

Of the above classes of men the *asthira* are the weakest. They do not understand the distinction between the proper and the improper, the more sinful and the less sinful, the commendable and what is not commendable, and are only given that form of penance which they themselves select, their attachment to the Path being enough expiation in their condition (Ś. 180—181).

The *nirpeksha* saints are ever vigilant and thoughtful; they immediately wipe off the stain of error, if any, by proper penance, undertaken in the presence of their own Self (*Atma*=soul). They observe the eight kinds of *śuddhi* (see Sannyāsa Dharma, pp. 56—60). They are all great yogis, endowed with the higher type of bony-formation and gifted with supreme composure; they do not trouble others for expiation and are competent to wash off the stain of evil action by themselves. They are generally purified by the mere confessing of a fault to themselves, though they may like to go through any and all other forms of expiation of their own free will. The *nirpeksha* may also confess to their preceptor and accept all kinds of expiation from him.

With reference to the *garvi* (proud) class of transgressors, he who is proud of his austerities and would prefer *tapa*-penance (fasting and the like) should be given the *chheda* (if that be the expiation merited) and *vice versa*. The *mṛidu* (meek) whose excessively unassuming nature does not suffer him to feel the humiliation involved in *chheda* (saluting freshly ordained saints first which is against the rule of seniority) should not be given that form of penance nor the *mūla*; he should be put on *tapa* (fasting, etc.) Similarly, he who has no faith in the efficacy of *chheda* (degrading) and *mūla* (re-ordination) should be put on *tapa*.

The *sāpeksha* confess their transgressions before their *āchārya*, and are given the first six forms of penance (namely, *ālochanā*, *pratikramaṇa*, *ubhaya*, *viveka*, *vyutsarga* and *tapa*); they do not need the remaining four, that is, *chheda*, *mūla*, *anupasthāpanā* and *pāranchika*.

The *agitārtha* (unillumined) does not deserve the *sthāpanā* group which comprise the *chheda*, the *mūla* and the *parihāra*. According to the practice of another order of Saints, he should be given nine out of the ten forms of penance, leaving out the *parihāra* (which they think is what is signified by the term *sthāpanā*).

The *alpaśruta* (or *alpavita*) should be given the *pancha kalyānaka* usually. Even if he has merited the *parihāra* (expulsion), he should only be given either the *chheda* or the *mūla* penance.

Regard must also be had to the penitent's bodily strength and mental composure in meting out expiation. The strong in body should be given all the ten kinds of penances. He who is easily upset or unsettled should be given such penances to do as will actually go to impart strength of will to him. The physically weak should be asked to do only that kind of penance which will keep up his strength. He who is lacking in bodily strength as well as in firmness of mind should be given even milder forms of penance than the last-named.

The man endowed with any of the last three types of bony formation (see the Practical Dharma), with bodily strength and much wisdom should be given all forms of *tapa*-penance—fasting and the like; but he should be given the *mūla* in place of the *parihāra* penance (if such be merited by him).

The *sarva-purṇa* is fit to be given all forms of penances. If he has, however, merited the *pāranchika* form, he should be given only the *anupasthāna* (*parihāra*). Even the *anupasthāna* penance he keeps in his own community (*sangha*) of saints and has not to be sent away to another community.

The wise *yogi* who is endowed with the learning comprised in nine *purvas* (departments of scriptural lore), imbued with faith, devoid of the sense of attachment and aversion for the worldly things, contented, not given to preaching, and filled with pure thoughts,—may be given the *anupasthāna* (expulsion) penance. The saint undergoing such a penance is, however, allowed to approach the leader of the *gaṇa* (community of saints) for asking him a question and for confession. He salutes and otherwise shows respect towards other saints; but they do not show him respect nor offer salutation.

Pāranchika penance is given to those saints who are endowed with great strength, with the higher type of bony formation, with faith, composure, renunciation, purity and other excellent virtues and who have also 'conquered' sleep. They differ from the *sarva-purṇa* only in so far as they are fully enlightened, given to preaching and do not need to sleep. Such a saint will not lose his spiritual purity even if he have to live away from the *sangha* (community of saints).

He who is guilty of the grossest of sins such as disrespect to the *Tirthamkara*, deserves the *pāranchika* (complete expulsion). He should go and live in places where there are no co-religionists of his. Really, *pāranchika* is only intended for him who is endowed with the very best and strongest type of bony-formation (the first, namely, *bajra-vṛiṣabha nārācha*)*, who is of strong character, enlightened with the knowledge of the ten *purvas* (departments of scriptural lore) and a preacher as well as the conqueror of the tendency to sleep. Such a person will not be 'lost' altogether even if he is turned out of the country and the *sangha*.

* See the Practical Dharma.

CHAPTER VI

THE SINFUL DISPOSITION

The following peculiarities of disposition are found to characterize the psychology of transgressors. A man would yield either under the stress of external circumstances (illness, compulsion and the like) or without such external stress; he may commit only one act of transgression or go on doing so; he may care to follow the Teaching of Truth, or he may not care to do so; and he may resist the downward step, or yield without resisting. This gives us a list of eight elements, or traits of character, which may be tabulated in four rows, as follows (the sign of + marking the element of goodness and that of – its antithesis):—

+ Yielding under stress (*sahetuka*).	1.	– yielding without external stress (*asahetuka*).
+ Stopping after one fault (*sakṛitakāri*).	2.	– committing more than one fault (*asakṛitakāri*).
+ Longing to follow the teaching of truth (*sānuvichi*).	3.	– not longing to follow the teaching of truth (*asānuvichi*).
+ Resisting the temptation (*prayatnavāna*).	4.	– not resisting the temptation (*aprayatnavāna*).

By combining these in different groups we get no less than 16 types of the transgressing disposition.

These are shown in the following tabulated form together with a set of arithmetical symbols to facilitate reference, the position of the symbols representing the row and the symbols (+ or −) themselves the affirmative or negative elements of character.

1. External stress, one fault, longing to live upto truth, resisting ... ... ++++
2. No external stress, one fault, longing to live upto truth, resisting ... −+++
3. External stress, repeated slips, longing to live upto truth, resisting ... +−++
4. No external stress, repeated slips, longing to live upto truth, resisting ... −−++
5. External stress, one fault, not longing to live upto truth, resisting ... ++−+
6. No external stress, one fault, not longing to live upto truth, resisting ... −+−+
7. External stress, repeated slips, not longing to live upto truth, resisting ... +−−+
8. No external stress, repeated slips, not longing to live upto truth, resisting ... −−−+
9. External stress, one fault, longing to live upto truth, not resisting ... +++−
10. No external stress, one fault, longing to live upto truth, not resisting ... −++−
11. External stress, repeated slips, longing to live upto truth, not resisting ... +−+−
12. No external stress, repeated slips, longing to live upto truth, not resisting ... −−+−
13. External stress, one fault, not longing to live upto truth, not resisting ... ++−−

14. No external stress, one fault, not longing to live upto truth, not resisting ... – + – –
15. External stress, repeated slips, not longing to live upto truth, not resisting ... + – – –
16. No external stress, repeated slips, not longing to live upto truth, not resisting... – – – –

Of these, the first is the best disposition, deserving of the lightest penance, and the last, the worst, which must be dealt with severely if the transgressor is to be reclaimed. Suitable penance should be prescribed for the remaining types, according to their enormity or mildness.

Generally speaking, the three affirmative elements in the last three out of the four rows are indicative of goodness of disposition; but in combination with the second element in the first row—yielding without external pressure—their value is considerably lessened. The three opposite traits in these rows naturally go to weaken the argument in favour of the natural goodness of the disposition. They have to be eradicated firmly, by severe penance. The total number of the combinations of the elements in the last three rows is eight, which may be put down as follows :—

1. One fault, longing to live upto truth, resisting.
2. Repeated slips, longing to live up to truth, resisting ... ...
3. One fault, no longing to live upto truth, resisting

4. Repeated slips, no longing to live upto truth, resisting ... ...
5. One fault, longing to live upto truth, non-resisting ... ...
6. Repeated slips, longing to live up to truth, non-resisting ... ...
7. One fault, no longing to live upto truth, non-resisting ... ...
8. Repeated slips, no longing to live upto truth, non-resisting ... ...

This shorter table of eight types will apply where the circumstances do not admit of the application of the principle of external compulsion or its antithesis or where severer penance is indicated, as will be seen later.

From another point of view, five elements have to be taken into consideration in determining the nature of the penance. These are: whether the transgressor is devoted to religion (*priya dharma*) or not (*apriya dharma*); whether he is endowed with much knowledge (*bahu jnāna*) or not (*alpa jnāna*); whether he committed the fault under external stress (*sahetuka*) or not (*asahetuka*); whether the transgression was confined to a single act (*sakṛitakāri*) or to a series of acts (*asakṛitakāri*); whether he is straightforward (*rijubhāva*) or not (*arijubhāva*). These should be arranged, as before, in five rows, and numbered, in the manner already pointed out. In this way we get $2^5 = 2\times2\times2\times2\times2 = 32$ types of sinful mentality. Naturally the penance for the best type which is to be symbolically represented by five plus marks (+++++) will be the lightest; but it will be the heaviest for the opposite kind (to be represented by the sign of *minus* repeated five times, thus −−−−−).

The technical term for the types (as well as for rows) is *aksha*; their tabulation is *prastāra*; the determination of the *aksha* from its position in the table is *naṣṭa*; and the determination of the position when the *aksha* is known is *uddiṣṭa*.

The 32 types are as follows:—

1.	Devoted, much learning, external pressure, one fault, straightforward ...	+++++
2.	Indifferent, much learning, external pressure, one fault, straightforward	−++++
3.	Devoted, little learning, external pressure, one fault, straightforward ...	+−+++
4.	Indifferent, little learning, external pressure, one fault, straightforward	−−+++
5.	Devoted, much learning, without external pressure, one fault, straightforward	++−++
6.	Indifferent, much learning, without external pressure, one fault, straightforward	−+−++

7. Devoted, little learning, without external pressure, one fault, straightforward ... ... + – – + +
8. Indifferent, little learning, without external pressure, one fault, straightforward ... ... – – – + +
9. Devoted, much learning, external pressure, repeated slips, straightforward + + + – +
10. Indifferent, much learning, external pressure, repeated slips, straightforward ... ... – + + – +
11. Devoted, little learning, external pressure, repeated slips, straightforward ... ... + – + – +
12. Indifferent, little learning, external pressure, repeated slips, straightforward ... ... – – + – +
13. Devoted, much learning, without external pressure, repeated slips, straightforward ... ... + + – – +
14. Indifferent, much learning, without external pressure, repeated slips, straightforward ... ... – + – – +
15. Devoted, little learning, without external pressure, repeated slips, straightforward ... ... + – – – +
16. Indifferent, little learning, without external pressure, repeated slips, straightforward ... ... – – – – +
17. Devoted, much learning, external pressure, one fault, not straightforward + + + + –

18. Indifferent, much learning, external pressure, one fault, not straightforward ... ... −+++−
19. Devoted, little learning, external pressure, one fault, not straightforward ... ... +−++−
20. Indifferent, little learning, external pressure, one fault, not straightforward ... ... −−++−
21. Devoted, much learning, no external-pressure, one fault, not straightforward ... ... ++−+−
22. Indifferent, much learning, no external pressure, one fault, not straightforward ... ... −+−+−
23. Devoted, little learning, no external pressure, one fault, not straightforward ... ... +−−+−
24. Indifferent, little learning, no external pressure, one fault, not straightforward ... ... −−−+−
25. Devoted, much learning, external pressure, repeated slips, not straightforward ... ... +++−−
26. Indifferent, much learning, external pressure, repeated slips, not straightforward ... ... −++−−
27. Devoted, little learning, external pressure, repeated slips, not straightforward ... ... +−+−−

28. Indifferent, little learning, external pressure, repeated slips, not straightforward ... ... – – + – –

29. Devoted, much learning, no external pressure, repeated slips, not straightforward ... ... + + – – –

30. Indifferent, much learning, no external pressure, repeated slips, not straightforward ... ... – + – – –

31. Devoted, little learning, no external pressure, repeated slips, not straightforward ... ... + – – – –

32. Indifferent, little learning, no external pressure, repeated slips, not straightforward ... ... – – – – –

The best method of remembering this table is to note that of the five features which figure in it, the first occurs alternately down the column; the second occurs in groups of two at a time, followed by its antithetical trait for two steps; the third occurs in groups of four at a time, followed by the antithesis to the extent of four steps; the fourth alternates after eight times, and the fifth, after sixteen steps. In a tabulated form the arrangement may be described as follows :

(1) First column	+-+-+-+-+-+-+-+-+-+-+-+-+-+-+-+-
(2) 2nd ,,	++--++--++--++--++--++--++--++--
(3) 3rd ,,	++++----++++----++++----++++----
(4) 4th ,,	++++++++--------++++++++--------
(5) 5th ,,	++++++++++++++++----------------

It should be known that the sign $+$ (*plus*) in the above diagram stands for the affirmative trait, and $-$ (*minus*) for its antithesis.

The rule for finding out the traits of character in any given position (that is, the *nasṭa*) is to posit the number of the position the combination of which is to be ascertained and to divide it by the number 2 for the trait of the first column which will be determined by the remainder, which may be one or nil. If the remainder be one, the attribute in question is of the affirmative type, otherwise its opposite. For the next column add one to the quotient if there be a remainder, but nothing if there be no remainder. The figure arrived at in this way is to be divided by 2 again, and the trait for the 2nd column to be determined as before. In this way the process is to be continued till the list is complete. Suppose we wish to ascertain the nature of the combination in the 15th position (in the table of 32 types). The process will be as follows:—

$\frac{15}{2}=7$ (1 remainder) = Devoted;

$\frac{7+1}{2}=4$ (no remainder) = Little learning;

$\frac{4}{2}=2$ (no remainder) = Without external pressure;

$\frac{2}{2}=1$ (no remainder) = Repeated slips;

$\frac{1}{2}=1$ remainder = Straightforward.

The method of finding out the position (*ud-diṣṭa*) of any particular combination of traits of character is this: begin by determining, with reference to the table giving the measure of alternations, the position of the attribute in the last column, then go on to the one next to it, and so on, till you get to the first, which will determine the number. Suppose we have to find out the position of the group "devoted, little knowledge, external pressure, one fault, not straightforward": we shall fix up the columns backwards, beginning with the last, thus

"not straightforward"	17—32	(does not occur in 1—16);
"one fault"	17—24	(does not occur in 25—32);
"external pressure"	17—20	(does not occur in 21—24);
"little knowledge"	19—20	(does not occur in 17—18);
"devoted"	19	(does not occur at 20).

This gives us the position of the combination in the above scheme as 19, which is correct. Another method of determining the position (*uddiṣṭa*) is this: write the figure 1 and then multiply it with 2 with reference to the trait of the last column; then deduct 1 from the total if the element be affirmative; then multiply the remainder again with two, with reference to the trait of the next preceding column, and deduct 1 as before, if it happens to be affirmative; repeat the process for the remaining columns till the first one is reached. The result will indicate the position which was to be determined.

Suppose we have to find out the position allotted to the "devoted, much learning, external pressure, one fault, straightforward" type: the process will be as follows:—

$1 \times 2 = 2 - 1 = 1$ with reference to the last column;

$1 \times 2 = 2 - 1 = 1$ with reference to the 4th column;

$1 \times 2 = 2 - 1 = 1$ with reference to the 3rd column;

$1 \times 2 = 2 - 1 = 1$ with reference to the 2nd column;

$1 \times 2 = 2 - 1 = 1$ with reference to the first column.

This gives us the answer that was sought, as the process ends here. To take another instance, suppose the type is "not-devoted, little-learning, no external pressure, repeated slips, straightforward." Then the process will be as follows:—

$1 \times 2 = 2 - 1 = 1$ (1 must be deducted as "straightforward" is an affirmative trait);

$1 \times 2 = 2$ (nothing to be deducted as "repeated slips" is an antithetical trait);

$2 \times 2 = 4$ with reference to the third column;

$4 \times 2 = 8$ with reference to the second column;

$8 \times 2 = 16$ with reference to the first column, which also contains the answer.

CHAPTER VII

CONSIDERATIONS AFFECTING PENANCE

1—Kāla (Time)

Considerations of time, place and local conditions influence the determination of penance.

Kāla, that is, time, has been divided into three classes, namely, the rainy season, winter and summer. In all the three *kālas* it is permissible to award severe, mild and middling forms of *tapa*. The severe *tapa* for the rainy season is five continuous fasts; that in winter is a four days' fast; and in summer a three days' fast at a stretch.

The middling *tapa* consists of four continuous fasts in the rainy season, three in winter, and two in summer.

The mild form of *tapa* signifies three days' continuous fasting in the rainy season, two days' in winter, and one day's in summer.

In all these fastings it is understood that only one meal is to be taken on the day preceding the commencement of the fast and on that on which it is broken.

There is another mode of classification of time which proceeds on the basis of the six recognized divisions of the year. These are:

(1) the *śarad*, that is, the months of *Asauja* and *Kārtika* = October and November (roughly);

(2) the *hemanta*, namely, the months of *Mārgśirṣa* and *Puṣa* = December and January (roughly);

(3) the *śiśira*, i.e., *Māgha* and *Phālguna* = February and March (roughly);

(4) the *vasanta*, i.e., the months of *Chaitra* and *Bysākha* = April and May (roughly);

(5) the *griṣma*, i.e., the months of *Jyeṣṭha* and *Aṣāḍha*, = June and July (roughly);

(6) the *varṣā*, i.e., the months of *Śrāvaṇa* and *Bhādrapada* = August and September (roughly).

Of these, the *śarad*, the *vasanta* and the *griṣma* are termed *guru*, and the rest *laghu*.

Tapa is also divided into *guru* (severe) and *laghu* (mild) types. By combining the elements of *guru* and *laghu* of *kāla* and *tapa* together, five combinations are obtained as follows:—

(1) *guru kāla* + *guru tapa*;

(2) *laghu kāla + laghu tapa*;
(3) *kāla guru + tapa laghu*,
or tapa guru + kāla laghu;
(4) *tapa guru + kāla* partly *laghu* and partly *guru*;
(5) *kāla guru + tapa* partly *laghu* and partly *guru*.

The Leader (*āchārya*) should award these in his discretion, according to the individual requirement and the condition of the seasons. In the *laghu kāla*, a *laghu* form of *tapa* should generally be given.

2—KSHETRA (Country)

Land is of ten kinds, broadly speaking—

(1) the *anūpa* which abounds in water, *e.g.*, Magadha (=Behar) and Malaya (Madura near the Western Ghats), Vanvāsa (Bengal), Konkan (the country lying to the east of the Western Ghats) and Sinddha (Sind);
(2) the *jāngala* (forest land) characterized by an abundance of insect life but not noted for much water;
(3) the *bhakta-kshetra*, the home of paddy;
(4) the *kalmāṣa kshetra* where the people grow various kinds of pulses chiefly;

(5) the *śaktū kshetra*, the land of barley, where people take *sattū* (a preparation of barley meal) generally;

(6) the *rasā pulāka* which is noted for milch cows and the abundance of the supply of milk and the products of milk;

(7) the *dhānya-pulāka*, the land of wheat and other kinds of cereals;

(8) the *yavāgū* where people take *yavāgū* (liquid foods, or paste-like *khichri**);

(9) the *kanda-kshetra*, where roots (potatoes of various kinds and other vegetables of the potato family) are grown;

(10) the *mūla*, where are grown chiefly such things as ginger, turmeric and other forms of pungent articles that grow underground.

The one rule in regard to the above places is this that light penance should be given in dry and hot places (like Marwad and Malwa) where rich food is not obtained. In colder places where plenty of milk and *ghee* is eaten by the people severe *tapa* is permissible.

3—FOOD-SUPPLY

In fixing the penance it is also necessary to bear in mind the nature of the food the penitents

* A dish of rice and *dal* (pulses) cooked together.

are likely to get. The general rule with regard to this is as follows: where the people, whether of one's own faith, or the followers of other creeds, are respectful and where the best of rich food is obtainable, severe *tapa* is indicated there; where the food obtainable is of a middling kind, less severe forms of penance should be enforced there; and where inferior kind of food, *e.g.*, cheap rice, is to be had, there the lightest penances, namely, *āchāmla*, *nirvikṛiti*, *purumandala* and *ekasthāna* are to be given, but not *upavāsa*.

CHAPTER VIII

THE PENANCES

1—Ālochanā (Confession)

Ālochanā means Confession.

There are ten faults of *ālochanā* which the confessing saint should avoid. These are as follows :—

1. *Ākampita*, bribing, *i.e.*, the offering of an acceptable present;
2. *Anumāpita*, pleading ill-health ; or taking advantage of a special occasion;
3. *Yaddṛiṣta*, concealing faults not perceived by others;
4. *Bādara*, non-observance of minor faults from laziness, or their concealment;
5. *Sūkṣama*, concealing major sins;
6. *Chhanna*, confession in the third person, *i.e.*, the endeavour to ascertain the proper penance, as if for some one else;
7. *Śabdākulita*, disclosing earlier sins;

8. *Bahujana*, questioning others about the (merit of the) penance prescribed by the *guru* (leader), or adopting what was prescribed for another as penance for one's own sins;
9. *Avyakta*, confessing before one of an equal status;
10. *Tatsevita*, confessing to oneself, *i.e.*, adopting the penance prescribed for some one else for the same kind of fault as one's own.

A confession is to be made before one's Leader (the *āchārya* of the community of saints). The ten kinds of faults mentioned above are to be avoided. All true facts should be disclosed before the leader.[1]

Ālochanā is enjoined as the proper and adequate penance for the following sins:—

for faults committed because of the natural imperfections in the performance of austerities and the control of the senses and the body and the mind;[2]

for the various forms of movements, however carefully executed, inasmuch as all movements are really opposed to the nature of pure spirit;[3]

for the movements performed with due care, whilst away from one's own community (of saints);[4]

[1] Ch. 162. [2] S'. 185. [3] S'. 186-187. [4] S'. 188.

for visiting another party of saints, though all faults are avoided when doing so.[1]

2—Pratikramaṇa

Pratikramaṇa means self-censure. It is adequate penance for the following faults: the utterance of venial untruths under the influence of sex-passion,[2] for throwing bodily products and excrement in places not intended for the purpose or in forbidden places,[3] for thinking evil, entertaining unbecoming thoughts, or showing disrespect, by the word of mouth, to the Founders of the Faith, the Gaṇadharas (Apostles of Tirthamkaras), or the Āchāryas and the like, and for resort to violence—kicking, beating, etc.,[4] for forgetting the *vaiyāvṛitya* (serving or nursing penance), sneezing, passing wind, yawning, dreaming evil dreams (nocturnal emission), or forgetting to attend on sickly saints,[5] for exhibiting visible marks of sexual excitement, whether seen by others or not, when walking, or when engaged in seeking or eating food,[6] and for exciting angry or painful feelings in the heart of another person.[7]

Pratikramaṇa should be performed immediately after the discovery of a fault, in language such

[1] S'. 189. [2] S'. 48. [3] S'. 48. [4] S'. 190. [5] S'. 192. [6] S'. 193. [7] S'. 193.

as this: Woe is me; I have wrought great evil; I disclaim my evil act; it is hereby annulled (disowned)! More severe forms of self-censure must be employed where such are indicated by the nature of the offence.

Repetition of the great Salutation *mantram* nine times is termed *laghu* (minor) *pratikramaṇa.* It should be performed generally after every sort of act, *e. g.*, eating, passing urine, etc., to avoid cultivating the sense of attachment or aversion to it.

3—TADUBHAYA

Tadubhaya is *ālochanā* (confession) plus self-censure (*pratikramaṇa*). It applies to cases of fine distinction which cannot be made by ordinary saints, on account of their natural deficiencies, or where faults are committed without being known, although due care is taken for observing the rules of conduct, especially of the processes of periodical—daily, nightly, fortnightly, four-monthly, yearly and death-bed—*pratikramaṇa*, as faultlessly as possible.[1]

4—VIVEKA

Viveka, also termed *Tyāga*, means giving up, that is discontinuing the action that was taking place. It is regarded as adequate penance in the following cases:—

[1] Ch. 192-194.

Where a dwelling place, food, or an article of use which was not deemed to be objectionable at first is discovered to be so later on;[1]

Where a doubt has arisen in the mind as regards the purity or objectionableness of the whole or a part of food;[2]

Where part of the food is found to be objectionable;[3]

Where the food is pure but unwholesome or unclean thoughts have become associated with the whole or a part of it;[4]

Where the mind is inclined to take food (prepared with all proper care) at night, owing to ill health or under the fear that one might not be able to get it again soon on account of famine;[5]

Where objectionable food or what has been given up is placed in the plate or hand, or where it has actually been put in the mouth.[6]

NOTE:—In cases where the objectionable article can be separated from the unobjectionable one, it is permissible to take the unobjectionable things and to leave the others (S'. 198-200).

5—KĀYOTSARGA

Such of the faults as are unavoidable or are com-

[1] S'. 197. [2] S'. 199. [3] S'. 198. [4] S'. 200. [5] S'. 201. [6] S'. 202.

monly committed and slight, *e.g.*, walking, eating, etc., only merit the *kāyotsarga* penance.[1] The same penance is indicated where an *apamṛiṣta* (untouchable or impure) body is touched, itching is relieved, or bodily limbs stretched or contracted, or where bodily products, (excrement, saliva, phlegm and the like) are discharged in a manner contrary to the proper mode.[2] *Kāyotsarga* is also the proper expiation for such acts as pulling threads or straw to pieces, causing slight agitation, the employment of hands in collecting books, mentally resolving to complete an *upkaraṇa* (an accessory, *e.g.*, a book or feather whisk) in a certain number of days.[3] If a bodily limb rub against clay, hard seeds, green grass or *tarasa* (insect) life, one *kāyotsarga* is the penance therefor.[4]

If a saint fail to observe the *kāyotsarga* penance at the proper time he incurs the penalty of an *upavāsa* (fast), but not of *chheda*.[5]

6—Tapa

Tapa generally means asceticism, but in connection with penance it signifies fasting.

One and thirty combinations are formed with the five types of fasting penances, namely, *puru-*

[1] S'. 28. [2] S'. 29. [3] S'. 30. [4] S'. 31. [5] S'. 210.

mandala, *nirvikriti*, *ekasthāna*, *āchāmla* and *upavāsa*, and along with *kāyotsarga*, which is the lightest form of penance, are provided for the thirty-two types of the sinful mentality, according to the degree of sinfulness. In this way different transgressors get suitable penance for their transgressions, and steady progress is maintained.

The thirty-one combinations of the five forms of fasting *tapa* are shown in the following table in which their values (see Chap. IV) are also shown. The first place is given to *kāyotsarga* naturally, as it is the lightest form of penance, and is to be prescribed for the mildest form of sin. The valuations arrived at are in terms of fractions or multiples of a fast.

				Value.
1.	Kāyotsarga	...	...	... *nil*
2.	Purumandala	...	...	... 0·25
3.	Nirvikriti	...	...	... 0·50
4.	Ekasthāna	...	...	... 0·50
5.	Āchāmla	...	...	... 0·75
6.	Upavāsa	...	...	... 1·0
7.	Nirvikriti	+ purumandala	...	... 0·75
8.	Ekasthāna	+ ,,	...	... 0·75
9.	Purumandala	+ āchāmla	...	... 1·0
10.	Ekasthāna	+ nirvikriti	...	.. 1·0
11.	Nirvikriti	+ āchāmla	...	... 1·25
12.	Ekasthāna	+ ,,	...	... 1·25
13.	Upavāsa	+ purumandala	...	... 1·25

No.	Combination				Value
14.	Uparasā	+nirvikṛiti	...	...	1·50
15.	„	+ekasthāna	...	...	1·50
16.	„	+āchāmla	...	...	1·75
17.	Purumandala	+nirvikṛiti	+ekasthāna	...	1·25
18.	„	+ „	+āchāmla	...	1·50
19.	„	+ekasthāna+	„	...	1·50
20.	„	+nirvikṛiti	+upavāsa	...	1·75
21.	„	+ekasthāna+	„	...	1·75
22.	Nirvikṛiti	+ „	+āchāmla	...	1·75
23.	„	+ „	+upavāsa	...	2·0
24.	Purumandala	+āchāmla	+ „	...	2·0
25.	Nirvikṛiti	+ „	+ „	...	2·25
26.	Ekasthāna	+ „	+ „	...	2·25
27.	Purumandala	+nirvikṛiti	+ekasthāna+ āchāmla	...	2·0
28.	Purumandala	+nirvikṛiti	+ekasthāna+ upavāsa	...	2·25
29.	Purumandala	+nirvikṛiti	+āchāmla	+upavāsa	2·50
30.	„	+ekasthāna+	„	+ „	2·50
31.	Nirvikṛiti	+ „	+ „	+ „	2·75
32.	„	+ „	+ „	+ „ +purumandala	3·0

The total number of the penances in the above 31 combinations is 80, which by the addition of one for a *kāyotsarga* becomes 81. The above table slightly differs from that given in the Hindi commentary, but, as already stated, the commentary is not critical. It even places *nirvikṛiti* which is equal to half a fast, before *purumandala* that is only a quarter of one. The explanation of the anomaly in the valuation of such of the combinations as the sixth (=one *upavāsa*) and the seventh (which is only equal to three-fourths of an *upavāsa*) is to be sought in the additional penances that are combined in the less valuable one, so that the one with the lower estimate is really the more difficult of the two, because of its observance being extended to a longer period (an extra day).

The (32) combinations are termed *ślākās* (purifications), and are to be distributed as follows amongst the 32 types of the sinful mentality (see Chapter VI *ante*) :—

TABLE (1)

Types	*Ślākās*	Purifications
1	*ālochanā* (simple confession)	mere confession
2	1st *ślākā*	one
3	2nd ,,	,,
4	3rd ,,	,,
5	4th ,,	,,
6	5th ,,	,,
7	6th ,,	two
8	7th ,,	,,
9	8th ,,	,,

Types	*Ślākās*	Purifications
10	9th *ślākā*	two
11	10th ,,	,,
12	11th ,,	,,
13	12th ,,	,,
14	13th ,,	,,
15	14th ,,	,,
16	15th ,,	,,
17	16th ,,	three
18	17th ,,	,,
19	18th ,,	,,
20	19th ,,	,,
21	20th ,,	,,
22	21st ,,	,,
23	22nd ,,	,,
24	23rd ,,	,,
25	24th ,,	,,
26	25th ,,	,,
27	26th ,,	four
28	27th ,,	,,
29	28th ,,	,,
30	29th ,,	,,
31	30th ,,	,,
32	31st ,,	five

As for the distribution of the *ślākās* with reference to the table of 16-typed sinful mentality, some *āchāryas* would seem to recommend the allotment of the first *ślākā* out of the original thirty-one (without counting *kāyotsarga* as one) to the first type, marked with four *plus* marks (++++), and of the rest to the remaining fifteen types—two to each type. In a tabulated form they may be shown, with their valuations, as follows:—

TABLE (2)

Types	*Ślākās*	Valuation
1	1st	0·25
2	2nd and 3rd	1·0
3	4th and 5th	1·75
4	6th and 7th	1·50
5	8th and 9th	2·0
6	10th and 11th	2·50
7	12th and 13th	2·75
8	14th and 15th	3·25
9	16th and 17th	2·75
10	18th and 19th	3·25
11	20th and 21st	3·50
12	22nd and 23rd	4·0
13	24th and 25th	4·50
14	26th and 27th	4·25
15	28th and 29th	5·0
16	30th and 31st	5·75

It will be seen that the above allotment is almost perfect, there being only two instances of irregularity which are, however, trifling, negligible and unavoidable. These purifications will fit even more judiciously in the revised table (see Table No. 4 *post*).

According to another method of calculation, *ālochanā* (confession) is to be allotted to the first type, and the distribution of the 32 *ślākās* is to be made as in the following table:—

TABLE (3)

Types	*Ślākās*	Purifications	Valuation
1	1 (only confession)	*ālochanā* (confession)	confession
2	2 (9th+26th)	6	3·0
3	2 (1st+2nd)	2	·75
4	2 (15th+30th)	6	4·50
5	2 (6th+13th)	4	2·25
6	2 (14th+27th)	6	3·75
7	2 (16th+22nd)	6	3·25
8	2 (12th+28th)	6	3·75
9	2 (3rd+4th)	2	1·25
10	2 (18th+20th)	6	3·25
11	2 (8th+11th)	4	2·25
12*	2 (21st+23rd)	6	3·75
13	2 (7th+10th)	4	2·0
14*	2 (24th+25th)	6	4·50
15	2 (17th+19th)	6	3·25
16	3 (5th+29th+31st)	10	6·50

* According to the text the *ślākās* allotted to the 10th type are the 21st and 23rd (with an estimated value of 3·75), and those allotted to the 12th are Nos. 18th and 20th (valued at 3·25). This is obviously wrong, as will be evident from an analysis of the estimation of the different elements of sinful mentality, according to which

repeated slip	is estimated at	0·75
not resisting	" " "	1·25
not longing to live upto truth	" " "	2·25
no external stress	" " "	3·0

At this valuation the penalty for the 12th type should be 3+·75+1·25=5; and for the 10th, 3+1·25=4·25. But according to the text 3·25 has been assigned to No. 12 and 3·75 to No 10. That some mistake has occurred in this connection in the text is evident from the fact that certain other writers (according to the Hindi commentary) allot the *ślākās* assigned to the 10th type to No. 14 and those assigned to the latter to No. 10. Against the seemingly lighter punishment in higher types of the negative order is to be set off the extended observance of penances, inasmuch as several *ślākās* are combined in the penance prescribed for those types.

If the types be re-arranged (in the proper way) the penalties will appear as follows :—

TABLE (4)

Types	Description	Signs	Valuation
1	One slip, resisting, longing to live upto truth, external stress	++++	confession
2	Repeated slips, resisting, longing to live upto truth, external stress ...	−+++	0.75
3	One slip, not resisting, longing to live upto truth, external stress	+−++	1.25
4	Repeated slips, not resisting, longing to live upto truth, external stress ...	−−++	2.25
5	One slip, resisting, not longing to live upto truth, external stress	++−+	2.25
6	Repeated slips, resisting, not longing to live upto truth, external stress ...	−+−+	3.25
7	One slip, not resisting, not longing to live upto truth, external stress ...	+−−+	2.0
8	Repeated slips, no resisting, not longing to live upto truth, external stress	−−−+	3.25
9	One slip, resisting, longing to live upto truth, no external stress	+++−	3.0
10	Repeated slips, resisting, longing to live upto truth, no external stress ...	−++−	4.50
11	One slip, not resisting, longing to live upto truth, no external stress ...	+−+−	3.25
12	Repeated slips, not resisting, longing to live upto truth, no external stress ...	−−+−	3.25
13	One slip, resisting, not longing to live upto truth, no external stress ...	++−−	3.75

Types	Description	Signs	Valuation
14	Repeated slips, resisting, not longing to live upto truth, no external stress ...	−+−−	3·75
15	One slip, not resisting, not longing to live upto truth, no external stress ...	+−−−	4·50
16	Repeated slips, not resisting, not longing to live upto truth, no external stress...	−−−−	6·50

If the scheme of the allotment of the *ślākās* is slightly revised, more satisfactory results will ensue. The following redistribution is likely to commend itself to a judicially trained mind:

TABLE (5)

Types	*Ślākās*	Valuation
1	Confession	No fasting value
2	2 (1st and 2nd)	0·75
3	2 (12th and 20th)	1·25
4	2 (7th and 10th)	2·0
5	2 (6th and 13th)	2·25
6	2 (8th and 11th)	2·25
7	2 (9th and 26th)	3·0
8	2 (16th and 22nd)	3·25
9	2 (17th and 19th)	3·25
10	2 (18th and 20th)	3·25
11	2 (14th and 27th)	3·75
12	2 (12th and 28th)	3·75
13	2 (21st and 23rd)	3·75
14	2 (15th and 30th)	4·50
15	2 (24th and 25th)	4·50
16	3 (5th, 29th and 31st)	6·50

NOTE.—Penances of the same face-value are not necessarily alike in point of merit and austerity.

With reference to the 8-typed classification the allotment of *ślākās* would be as follows:—

TABLE (6)

Types	*Ślākās*	Purifications	Valuation
1	3 (1st, 2nd and 3rd)	3	1·50
2	4 (4th, 5th, 6th and 13th)	6	4·0
3	4 (7th, 8th, 14th and 15th)	8	5·0
4	4 (9th, 10th, 11th and 12th)	8	4·75
5	4 (16th, 18th, 23rd and 25th)	12	7·0
6	4 (17th, 19th, 20th and 24th)	12	7·25
7	4 (21st, 22nd, 26th and 30th)	14	8·50
8	4 (27th, 28th, 29th and 31st)	17	10·25

NOTE.—It is to be borne in mind that the types marked by odd numbers are generally less evil, than the next even ones, though amongst themselves they become more worthy of censure as we rise higher, thus the seventh is the worst in this class, the fifth more evil than the third but less than the seventh, and so forth. The same remark applies to those marked by even numbers as regards their comparative sinfulness.

It should be noted that the tables of penances given above are characterised by rising severity of expiation, and mark the limits of the maximum and the minimum of penance for faults committed. The penalty is to be fixed with due regard to all the considerations that may present themselves in individual cases. It should never be forgotten that the object of penance is the re-establishing of the penitent in the very position of purity from which he has fallen. Punishment may be the object in the view of the temporal judge; it is not in that of the Spiritual Leader!

The thirty-one forms of the fasting penance may be combined with other kinds of penance, *kāyotsarga*, *pratikramaṇa* and the like, in the discretion of the Leader (*āchārya*), according to the requirements of the individual cases.

The limit for the fasting penance, strictly speaking, is six months. If it is prolonged it might produce ill effect, and may lead to evil thinking and disrespect in the mind of the penitent and others, which must be avoided in any case. If the sinner be incorrigible and not amenable to penance, or his sin be something that is likely to bring unprecedented trouble on the community of saints, the remedy is expulsion; but not the imposition of unbearable *tapa* (fasting). However, some *āchāryas* have recommended severer fasting in the case of nuns who have misbehaved with saints or other men. The limit in such a case would be seven months. He who kills a Jaina saint has, however, to observe 2-days' fasts for a whole year.[1]

[1] Ch. 11.

The method of observing the *ślākās* is two-fold: with intervals, that is, by the interposition of regular meals, termed *sāntara*, and without such interposition (*nirantara*). The order of observance in the first case (*e.g.* with reference to *nirvikṛiti*) will be as follows: *nirvikṛiti*, regular meal, *nirvik.*, regular meal, *nirv.*, reg. meal,......and so on. In the other case it will be: *nirvikṛiti*, *nirv.* n, n, . . . and so on. Whether it be *purumandala*, *nirvikṛiti*, *ekasthāna*, *āchāmla* or *upavāsa*, the order will be the same for every one of them.

In observing the combinations also the same method is to be followed. If it is *sāntara* observance, a regular meal will be allowed after the combination, which in itself will not be broken up, *e.g.*, *purumandala*, *nirvikṛiti*, *ekasthāna*, *āchāmla*, *upavāsa*, regular meal, *purumandala*, *nirvikṛiti*, *ekasthāna*, *āchāmla*, *upavāsa*, regular meal......and so on.

If the observance is without the interposition of regular meals, the combinations will run on without break, till the whole period during which the penance is to be observed is gone through.

7—Chheda

Chheda is the loss of seniority measured by days, fortnights, months, and years. He who does not improve in any other way, that is, by milder measures, must be treated with *chheda.* It is also given for those who have merited severer penance than fasting, but who have not deserved reordination (*mūla*).

The following are some of the occasions for the enforcement of this form of penance :—

Faults.	Period of *chheda.*
For leaving the *sangha* (company of saints) and for moving about alone[1]	As much time as the penitent has lived away.
For falling away from the true saintly path, and roaming about in different unsaintly or less saintly (lax) styles[2]	As much time as the transgressor remains away from the true saintly path.
For keeping the company of unsaintly *sādhus* by one who pulls himself up readily again after a slip	
(1) if he return within six months	Tapa penance ;
(2) if after six months[3]	Chheda (for the whole length of the period of absence).
For failure to apologise after a fault (when the saint remains in the *sangha*)	
(1) in the case of an ordinary saint	5 days for every 24 hours' delay ;
(2) for a specially qualified or learned saint	10 days for every 24 hours' delay ;
(3) for an *āchārya*[4]	15 days for every 24 hours' delay.
For leaving the *sangha* without apologising for the fault committed.	
(1) for an ordinary saint	10 days for every 24 hours' delay ;
(2) in the case of an advanced or specially qualified saint	15 days for every 24 hours' delay ;
(3) in the case of an āchārya[5]	20 days for every 24 hours' delay.

[1] Ś. 227. [2] Ś. 228—229. [3] Ś. 230. [4] Ś. 231—232. [5] Ś. 233.

8—MŪLA

So long as *chheda* is still available as a penance and *mūla* has not been merited by the transgressor, *chheda* should be given. *Mūla* signifies complete deprivation of seniority and amounts to re-ordination. He who is given this form of penance will not rank as senior to a saint who is ordained just at that moment. For such faults as are beyond the curative efficacy of the *chheda*, that is to say, which are too grave to be cured by it and yet are not strong enough to merit *parihāra* (expulsion), the proper penance is *mūla*. If the *mahā-vratas* (the main vows of asceticism) have been violated completely the proper penance is *mūla* (to establish the delinquent once more in the vows). It should be sought from the same *āchārya* who originally ordained the transgressor.[1]

The *mūla* is indicated, as the proper penance, in the following cases :—

For the loss of faith, conduct and the principal vows, and for the non-observance of the six necessary daily duties, and for ordaining a pregnant woman or an impotent person into sainthood.[2]

For propounding doctrines which are opposed to the Teaching of the Scripture.[3]

[1] Ch. 112. [2] Ś. 237. [3] Ś. 238.

For behaving in unsaintly or lax, *i.e.*, less-saintly modes, that is, for adopting the life of a *pārsvastha, kuśila, avasanna, or mṛigchāri* sādhu.[1]

For adopting the mode and style of the *sādhus* of the non-Jaina faiths, for falling back into the householder's stage, for insincerity in the adoption of the vows of a Jaina saint, and for very gross sins.[2]

For the commission of sins that are destructive of the *mūla guṇas* (root virtues) of saintly life, and for ordaining men of the *pariah* caste.[3]

NOTE.—Those who have been admitted into the order by any of the unsaintly saints named in the 239th *śloka* should be admitted into the order by *mula* (re-ordination).

If a saint loses faith in the doctrine of truth, but reverts to the true faith himself without any one's knowing of his loss of faith, he may select his own penance (whatever he likes); but if his change of belief becomes known to any one, then he should be given the *mūla* penance.[4]

9—PARIHĀRA

Parihāra (expulsion) is either partial or complete. Partial expulsion from the *sangha* (the company to which one belongs) is *anupasthāna* or *anupasthāpanā parihāra.* There are two types of

[1] Ś. 239. [2] Ś. 240. [3] Ś. 241 [4] Ś. 253—254.

this: *sva-gaṇa* (own *gaṇa*) *anupasthāpanā*, and *paragaṇa* (another *gaṇa*) *anupasthāpanā*. *Gaṇa* means the same thing here as a company of saints. The difference between these two types lies in this that while in the *sva-gaṇa* the penitent remains attached to his own *gaṇa*, and takes absolution from his own Leader, in the *para-gaṇa* type he is sent from leader to leader, and, required to confess his sin to at least three *āchāryas* of different *sanghas*, and in the more heinous cases, to as many as seven *āchāryās*. He is then sent back to his own *āchārya*, either in the backward order or direct, and from him he takes his penance.

The *sva-gaṇa* penitent sits at a distance of 64 yards from his *sangha* and has to salute, attend on and serve the juniormost members of it. Even if a junior saint come his way he must stand up and advance towards him, to show him respect; but he is not entitled to be treated with this mark of respect from his juniors under similar circumstances. He must devote his time to the observance of the penance, seated outside the gathering of his brother saints at a proper distance. The penitent is also required to observe fasting of the severest type, the mildest being one regular meal after every five days' fast, and the severest, after every six months; which is beyond the capacity of the present-day humanity, though not of the men of the adamantine frames of the hoary past. The penance may have to be observed for a period of 12 years.

Pāranchika parihāra is deserved by those whose sins are the blackest and the worst. The sinner in this case has his sin proclaimed before the world, is turned out of the country and may have to live even among strangers and men of wrong faiths. He is required to observe the fasting penance as in the *anupasthāpanā parihāra*, with the same types of severity and for a similar period, namely, 12 years. Then he will be deemed to have been purified and absolved.

Anupasthāpanā is indicated in the following cases :—

For the abduction of a *sādhu* of another faith, or of a layman, a woman, a child or the pupil of a brother saint, and for assaulting or striking a saint with a stick.[1]

Pāranchika parihāra is provided for men who show disrespect to and insult the Tirthamkaras, the Siddhas and Holy Saints, or who join the king's enemies.[2] It is also the penalty incurred by those who defile the True Faith and the Scripture of Truth.[3] He who is an enemy of the ruling king,

[1] Ś. 245. [2] Ś. 249. [3] S. 250.

or who ordains the experienced officers of the state when their services are indispensable for the public good also deserves the *pāranchika parihāra.*[1] The defiler or the lover of the *pattarāni* (chief queen) is also worthy of the severest penalty known to the *āchārya* judge.[2]

10—Śraddhāna

Śraddhāna signifies the acquisition of faith. It is applicable to the case of a renegade or apostate who wishes to come back into the Right Fold once more. He may be re-admitted into the order of the saints in the discretion of the Leader (*āchārya*) if he is able to observe the *mūla guṇas* (root virtues) of sainthood.

[1] S. 250. [2] S. 250.

PART II

PENANCES

1—Concerning the First Vow (Ahimsā)

To determine the amount of the proper penance merited by a saint for the destruction of the life of different kinds of living beings, a reference has to be made to the "senses and *prāṇas*" with which different forms of life are endowed differently.

The lowest form of life is one-sensed, which comprises those living beings who are endowed only with the sense of touch, *e.g.*, vegetables. Then there are the two-sensed beings, who enjoy touch and taste both, as is the case with oysters and snails. The three-sensed have smell in addition to the above two. In this class are found ants and many other kinds of insects. In the class of four-sensed life are included bees and flies, etc. They have sight also. The five-sensed are the fishes, rats, monkeys, man, etc. They enjoy hearing also. In this class there are two sub-divisions, the *sangi* (endowed with the capacity to think) and the *asangi* (not capable of rational thought).

As regards *prāṇas* (vitalities), the one-sensed have four of them, namely, breath, bodily strength, longevity and the sense of touch. The two-sensed have these four, and in addition they have the sense of taste and the capacity to utter sounds. The three-sensed have the sense of smell, the four-sensed those of smell and sight, and the five-sensed those of smell, sight and hearing in addition to the six possessed by the two-sensed. Then the *sangi* five-sensed beings are further endowed with the organ of thought. We thus have five senses and ten *prāṇas*, which are the basis of the discriminating treatment of the different kinds of sinners.

The mildest form of penance is to require one *kāyotsarga* for each sense, so that if a one-sensed form of life is destroyed one *kāyotsarga* is the penance therefor. For a two-sensed insect, two *kāyotsargas* are necessary, and so on.

Severer forms of penance are provided with reference to the mental characteristics of the sinner. The elements taken into consideration, according to one method of calculation, are the following:

1. whether observing fundamental virtues (*mūla guṇas*) only or additional ones (*uttara guṇas*) also;

2. whether inclined to resist temptation or sinning (*prayatnachāri*) or not (*aprayatnachāri*);

3. whether wavering (*asthira*) in the observance of the rules, or unwavering (*sthira*).

By combining them differently we get the following eight types of mentality :—

1.	*Uttara* g.	+ resisting	+ unwavering	
2.	*Mūla* g.	+ "	+ "	
3.	*Uttara* g.	+ unresisting	+ "	
4.	*Mūla* g.	+ "	+ "	
5.	*Uttara* g.	+ resisting	+ wavering	
6.	*Mūla* g.	+ "	+ "	
7.	*Uttara* g.	+ unresisting	+ "	
8.	*Mūla* g.	+ "	+ "	

The penance proper for the destruction of different forms of animal life is shown in the following table. In this table *K* stands for a *Kāyotsarga* and *K/u* for one *Kāyotsarga* and one *upavāsa* (fast).

Serial number.	Temperament.	one-sensed		2-sensed		3-sensed		4-sensed		5-sensed: unable to think		5-sensed: able to think	
		sense 1	vitalities 4	senses 2	vitalities 6	senses 3	vitalities 7	senses 4	vitalities 8	senses 5	vitalities 9	senses 5	vitalities 10
1	*Uttara g.* + resisting + unwavering	1 k		2 k		3 k		4 k		5 k		5 k	
2	*Mūla g.* + resisting + unwavering	1 k		2 k		3 k		4 k		5 k		5 k	
3	*Uttara g.* + unresisting + unwavering	1 k/u		2k/u		3k/u		4 k/u		5 k/u		5 k/u	
4	*Mūla g.* + unresisting + unwavering	1 k/u		2k/u		3k/u		4 k/u		5 k/u		5 k/u	
5	*Uttara g.* + resisting + wavering		4 k		6 k		7 k		8 k		9 k		10 k
6	*Mūla g.* + resisting + wavering		4 k		6 k		7k		8 k		9 k		10 k
7	*Uttara g.* + unresisting + wavering		4 k/u		6 k/u		7 k/u		8 k/u		9 k/u		10 k/u
8	*Mūla g.* + unresisting + wavering		4 k/u		6 k/u		7 k/u		8 k/u		9 k/u		10 k/u

According to some *āchāryas* the resisting type of personality is entitled to be treated on the basis of the senses destroyed, and the unresisting on that of vitalities. Fasting is to be added on the following basis: for the destruction of 12 one-sensed forms of life one fast. Further equations are as follows:—

12 1-sensed lives = 6 2-sensed ones = 4 3-sensed ones = 3 4-sensed ones. If destruction of life has taken place on a larger scale the equation will not be observed. But for 36 one-sensed lives two continuous fasts are required to be observed. Two continuous fasts are also required for 18 2-sensed, 12 3-sensed, 9 4-sensed and 1 5-sensed forms of life.

According to another method the table of penances is to be worked out as follows:—

	Types of temperament.	Destruction of all forms of life except that endowed with the capacity to think (the *sangi*).	
		for one sin	for repeated sins
1	*Uttara g.* + unwavering + vigilant	*1 kalyānaka*	*3 upavāsas*
2	*Mūla g.* + unwavering + vigilant	*2 upavāsas**	*3 upavāsas*

* According to the text the penance for one fault in this case is 3 *upavāsas* and for repeated faults only 2 *upavāsas*; but this is a clear case of error. The necessary correction has therefore been made in this place.

	Types of temperament.	Destruction of all forms of life except that endowed with the capacity to think (the *sangi*).	
		for one sin	for repeated sins
3	*Uttara g.* + wavering + vigilant	*1 kalyānaka*	*1 kalyānaka*
4	*Mūla g.* + wavering + vigilant	*2 upavāsas*	*1 pancha kalyānaka*
5	*Uttara g.* + unwavering + non-vigilant	*2 upavāsas**	*3 upavāsas**
6	*Mūla g.* + unwavering + non-vigilant	*2 upavāsas*	*1 kalyānaka*
7	*Uttara g.* + wavering + non-vigilant	*2 upavāsas*	*1 pancha kalyānaka*
8	*Mūla g.* + wavering + non-vigilant	*laghumāsa (one kalyānaka)*	*mūla*

The same is the penance for the destruction of the *sangi* type of the 5-sensed forms of animal-life, except that the fasts are then required to be observed without interruption, whereas in the other case regular meals are allowed to be interposed between fasts, in case of illness.

Some *āchāryas* divide the motive for an action into two classes and then subdivide each of them into different sub-classes as follows:—

* According to the text the penance for one fault in this case is *3 upavāsas* and for repeated faults only *2 upavāsas*; but this is covered by the remark in the foot-note on the preceding page, and has been corrected as before.

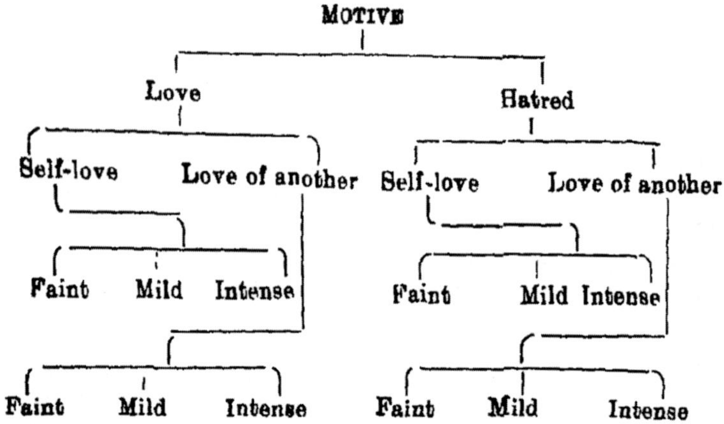

Hatred is always evil, and the same is the case with self-love (selfishness). The love of another, which manifests itself in acts of sympathy, philanthropy and the like, is commendable in the householder's stage; but it has to be given up in *sannyāsa*. Nevertheless the penance for the doing of an act of sympathy is rather mild as compared with that for a selfish one.

Further forms of penance in connection with the first vow (*ahimsā*) are given below:—

For causing the death of a Jaina Saint[1]	2-days' fasts for a whole year.
For causing the death of a Jaina layman[1]	ditto for 6 months.
For causing the death of a child[1] ...	ditto for 3 months.
For causing the death of a woman ...	ditto for 1½ months.
For causing the death of a *sadhu* of another faith[2]	ditto for 6 months.

[1] Ch. 11. [2] Ch. 12.

For causing the death of a pious layman of another persuasion[1] ...	2-days' fasts for 3 months.
For causing the death of an ordinary individual[1]	ditto for 1½ months.
For causing the death of a Brāhmana[2] ...	ditto for 8 months.
For causing the death of a Kshatriya[2] ...	ditto for 4 months.
For causing the death of a Vaiśya[2] ...	ditto for 2 months.
For causing the death of a Śudra[2] ...	ditto for 1 month.
For causing the death of a quadruped[2] ...	ditto for ½ month.
For causing the death of a herbivorous animal[3]	14 one-day fasts.
For causing the death of a beast of prey[3]	13 one-day fasts.
For causing the death of a bird[3] ...	12 one-day fasts.
For causing the death of a serpent[3] ...	11 one-day fasts.
For causing the death of a poisonous serpent[3]	10 one-day fasts.
For causing the death of a crocodile, fish, etc.[3]	9 one-day fasts.

NOTE.—In observing the fasts and two-days' fasts, a regular meal is deemed to be interposed between two fasting periods. Where two-days' fasts are enjoined, for a long period, the process must begin and end with one such fast (*i.e.*, a two-days' fast, termed *belā*).

For cutting or piercing green grass or leaves but once[4]	one *purumandala*.
For cutting or breaking a multi-souled vegetable organism[4]	one *āchāmla*.
For causing hurt to insect life[4] ...	one *ekasthāna*.
For causing injury to ordinary vegetable life, through lack of vigilance[4] ...	one *āchāmla*.
For the above if multi-souled vegetable life is harmed[5]	one *ekasthāna*.

[1] Ch. 12. [2] Ch. 13. [3] Ch. 14. [4] Ś. 33. [5] Ś. 34.

For causing injury if insect life is harmed[1] one *upavāsa*.

For the death of an insect in the saint's gourd if he be on the 7th stage[2] ... five *nirvikṛitis*.

if he be on the 6th stage[2] ... ... one *kalyānaka*.

For the repeated death of insects in the gourd[3] ... ... one *pancha kalyānaka*.

For the destruction of the life of a five-sensed insect whether through carelessness or otherwise, that is to say, even in spite of ordinary care, for the first fault[3] ... ... one *kalyānaka*.

For the death of a five-sensed insect on the plank (bed)[3]... ... ... one *kalyānaka*.

For the above when the saint was careful in his movements[3] ... ... five *nirvikṛitis*.

For the death of a five-sensed animal in the lower part of the door of the *bastikā* (dwelling for the night)[4] ... one *kalyānaka*.

NOTE.—This is the penance for every saint who has gone in or come out of such a *bastikā*.[4]

For being the occasion of the death of a five-sensed living being, such as a (wild) cat, or a centipede, having drawn the attention of its destroyer to its presence—

(*i*) if the language of the saint was calm and did not show alarm[5] ... one *upavāsa*.

(*ii*) if he was alarmed or showed alarm[5] one *pancha kalyānaka*.

NOTE.—No penance is incurred if the saint merely said there is a poisonous snake, or words to that effect and some one immediately killed it, to protect those present.[5]

1 Ś. 34. 2 Ś. 35-36. 3 Ś. 37. 4 Ś. 38. 5 Ś. 39—41.

2—CONCERNING THE SECOND VOW (TRUTHFULNESS).

For direct falsehood[1]	one *kāyotsarga*, one fast and *pratikramaṇa.*
For an indirect lie[1]	two *kāyotsargas*, two fasts and *pratikramaṇa.*
For both (the above) combined[1] ...	three *kāyotsargas*, three fasts and *pratikramaṇa.*
For thinking, speaking and acting a lie[1] ...	four *kāyotsargas*, four fasts and *pratikramaṇa.*
For repeated falsehood through excitement of passions[2]	one *pancha kalyānaka.*
For repeated falsehood at the instance of another.[2]	multiples of the combinations of *kāyotsargas*, fasts and *pratikramaṇa*, not exceeding one *māsika* (*pancha kalyānaka*).
For the habit of lying in an evil-minded saint[3]	*parihāra* of both kinds (expulsion from the *sangha* and the country).

NOTE.—If any saint treat the lie uttered by another saint as truth he is deemed to participate in the lie to the extent of a fourth part.

For the utterance of venial untruths under the influence of sexual passion[4] ...	*pratikramaṇa.*

[1] Ch. 15. [2] Ch. 16. [3] Ch. 17. [4] Ś. 48.

3—Concerning the Third Vow (non-Stealing).

For taking what has not been given by its owner—

(*i*) if done in a deserted plače and without any concealment[1] ...	one *kāyotsarga*, one *upavāsa* and *pratikramaṇa*.
(*ii*) if in the presence of one's own companions[1]	two *kāyotsargas*, two fasts and *pratikramaṇa*.
(*iii*) if in the presence of men of other faiths[1]	three *kāyotsargas*, three fasts and *pratikramaṇa*.

For repeated failings in this respect[1] one *pancha kalyānaka*.

Note.—On the death of an *āchārya* or saint, his whisk and gourd and books descend to his disciple, and in his absence to the deceased's co-pupil. If there is no co-pupil, then they go to the saints in his *gachcha* (a group of three saints). In any case they will go to the *sangha* (a group of seven saints).[2] Any saint may accept a gift (of a permissible article) from any other saint, whether belonging to his *gaṇa* or *gachha*, or not; but the books are intended only for the learned.[3] They will, however, go to whomsoever they are given by the owner.[3] If any saint unlawfully possess himself of what he is not entitled to take under the above rule, he is liable to be deprived of the article and to undergo a *tapa* penance which might extend to six months' continuous fasting.[4] This rule will apply even though there be a decision by a king or a court of law to the contrary. The delinquent may also be required to maintain silence throughout the whole period of fasting.[4]

For helping oneself, that is, taking when not actually given—

[1] Ch. 18. [2] Ch. 19. [3] Ch. 20. [4] Ch. 21-22.

(*i*) a book or books ... ... one *laghumāsa.*
(*ii*) a feather whisk ... ... one *kalyānaka.*
(*iii*) a gourd or any other object of the lowest type of utility[1] ... one *purumandala.*

For damaging or taking without the owner's permission such things as thorns, bricks, wood, tiles, ashes, and cow-dung[2] ... ... one *kalyānaka.*

For taking what has been given for the use of another saint[3] ... ... one *pancha kalyānaka.*

4—Concerning the Fourth Vow (Celibacy).

For evil dreams, that is nocturnal emission[4] ... ... *pratikramaṇa.*

For dreaming bad dreams (nocturnal emission) after midnight[5] ... ... *a kāyotsarga.*

For evil dreams (*i.e*, emission of semen) during the first watch of the night—

(*a*) if the saint had gone to sleep after performing meditation, self-examination and adoration ... ... *pratikramaṇa*;

(*b*) if after doing any two of the above ... ... one *upavāsa*+mild *pratikramaṇa.*

(*c*) if after only one of the above[6] one *upavāsa*+*pratikramaṇa.*

For the same fault when it is committed in the last watch[7]

for (*a*) ... ... *Pratikramaṇa*+ 2. days' fast (*belā*).

for (*b*) ... ... one *upavāsa*+*pratikramaṇa.*

[1] Ś. 123. [2] Ś. 214. [3] Ś. 126. [4] Ś. 192. [5] Ś. 203. [6] Ch. 23.
[7] Ch. 24.

for (c) ... . *niyama* (mild self-censure)+ *upavāsa.*

For dreaming of indulging in sexual intercourse, meat, wine or honey—

(a) if this happen only once ... one *upavāsa.*

(b) if it happen repeatedly[1] ... *pratikramaṇa* + *upavāsa,*

For chatting with a young woman when the saint happen to be young himself—

(a) if it happen only once ... one fast.

(b) if it happen repeatedly[2] ... a number of fasts which might extend alternately up to six months.

For the above when committed in secret after a warning in that regard from the preceptor[3] ... ... one or more *ṣaṣṭhas* up to six months; in the worst cases *parihāra* (expulsion) may have to be tried; but if the transgressing saint wishes to live in the *sangha* the leader may require him to observe the vow of silence for six months or even longer, repenting for his misdeed.

For the feeling of excitement when looking at a woman's face or bodily limbs[4] *alochanā* + *kāyotsarga.*

For trying to behold a woman's nakedness, or for the use of exciting *rasas*

[1] Ch. 25 [2] Ch. 26. [3] Ch. 27-28. [4] Ś. 30.

(sugar, milk, *ghee*, etc.)[1]	avoidance of *rasas* + *swādhyāya*[2] + recitation of the holy salutation *mantram* + contemplation of the divine form.
For misbehaving (having sexual intimacy) with a nun[3]	Expulsion.

NOTE.—The nun cannot be reclaimed according to the Chulika; but the saint can be purified by undergoing specially apportioned penance if he be sincerely sorry for his error. But he should live in a country where the people do not know of his misdeed, and, therefore, do not despise him. In the Purāṇas, however, there is the example of Jaiṣṭhā, the nun, who was re-admitted into the order after giving birth to an illegitimate child. But this was when Mahavira was Himself living on earth!

For exhibiting visible marks of sexual excitement when walking, whether seen by others or not[4]	*pratikramaṇa*.
For exhibiting visible marks of sexual excitement when engaged in seeking or eating food[4]	*pratikramaṇa*.
For re-entertaining sex-longing, in intenser form, after once regretting it[5] ...	one *pancha kalyānaka*.
For actually indulging in sexual intercourse under the above circumstances[5]	alternate fasts for a period of four months.
For the use of medicines to strengthen or beautify the body[6]	one *pancha kalyānaka*.
For uttering venial untruths under the influence of sex-passion[7] ...	*pratikramaṇa*.

[1] Ś. 31. [2] *Swādhyāya* means scriptural study. [3] Ch. 126—129. [4] Ś. 191. [5] Ś. 65. [6] Ś. 65. [7] Ś. 48.

For stroking the private parts or pressing the sexual organ between the thighs or legs[1]	one *kalyānaka.*
For sexual indulgence under external compulsion[2]	one *pancha kalyānaka.*

NOTE.—There is no penance if a saint sleep between two women provided his heart remains unaffected by the virus of desire.

For the emission of semen on account of excessive sexual craving (masturbation?)[2]	one *pancha kalyānaka.*

5—CONCERNING THE FIFTH VOW (POSSESSION-LESSNESS).

For keeping the paraphernalia of a householder[3]	one fast.
For covetousness for gold, silver, etc.[3]	a two-days' fast.
For obtaining gold, silver, etc., by begging[3]...	a three-days' fast.
For receiving valuable things on the occasions of eclipses, or planetary changes and the like[3]	one *māsika.*
For collecting silver and gold and the like at one's pleasure[3]	*mūla.*
For using any kind of clothes[4] ...	one *kalyānaka.*
For using any kind of skins[4] ...	one *kalyānaka.*
For using any kind of support or seat other than a wooden plank or a wooden or stone seat[5]	one *kalyānaka.*

[1] Ś. 214. [2] Ś. 116. [3] Ś. 114. [4] Ś. 50 and 73. [5] S. 50 and 73.

6—Concerning the First Samiti (Travelling and Walking).

For walking (for exercise) one mile along an insect-free path[1] ... ... one *kāyotsarga*.

For walking (for exercise) one mile along a path that is not insect-free[1]... ... one *upavāsa*.

For walking during the day time along an insect-free path, as far as six miles in the rainy season, 12 in winter, and 18 in summer[2] .. .. one *upavāsa*.

For walking during the day time along a path that is not insect-free, if the distance amount to 4 miles in the rainy season, 8 in winter, and 12 in summer[3] ... one *upavāsa*.

For walking at night in the rainy season along an insect-free path, if the distance covered be 6 miles[3] ... ... one 3-days' fast.

For walking 6 miles at night in the rainy season along a path that is not insect-free[3] ... ... one 4-days' fast.

For walking at night a distance of eight miles along an insect-free path in the winter season[3] ... ... one 2-days' fast.

For walking in winter at night a distance of eight miles along a path that is not insect-free[3] ... ... one 3-days' fast.

For walking 12 miles in summer at night along an insect-free path[3] ... one *upavāsa*.

For walking 12 miles in summer at night when the path trodden is not insect-free[3] one 2-days' fast.

For walking or passing through water[4] some severe form of penance.

For passing through water at a regular ford, if not more than knee-deep[5] ... one *kāyotsarga*.

[1] Ch. 34. [2] Ch. 35. [3] Ch. 36-37. [4] Ch. 42. [5] Ch. 39.

For passing through water when the water is four fingers' breadth above the knees[1]	One *upavāsa*.
For every additional 4 fingers' breadth (of water)[1]	double the number of fasts.
For passing through water at a place where there is no ford[1]	severer forms of *kāyotsarga* and fasts.

NOTE.—There is no penance for crossing the water at a ford where it is not longer than 32 yards, and is free from the water fauna.[2]

For crossing a stream in a boat, whether built for one's own use or not[3] ...	One *kāyotsarga* and *ālochanā*.
For crossing a stream in an aggravated case[3]	one *kāyotsarga* and one *upavāsa*.
For crossing a sea in a boat[3] ...	one *upavāsa* (and may be one *kalyānaka*).
For travelling in a palanquin or vehicle[4]	twice the penance provided for walking.
For travelling without the feather whisk[5]	
(*a*) when the distance covered does not exceed 7 paces	one *kāyotsarga*.
(*b*) when it does not exceed 2 miles (=1 *kosa*)...	one *upavāsa*.
(*c*) for every additional *kosa* thereafter...	double the number of fasts.
For travelling along an improper or unauthorised path, or for passing over green grass or fresh leaves[6]	one *kāyotsarga*.

[1] Ch. 39. [2] Ch. 40. [3] The Chheda Pinda (1-2). [4] Ch. 43. [5] Ch. 44. [6] Ś. 203.

For crossing a stream, pond or lake in a boat, when no payment is made, and when the boat was made without reference to the saint's need[1] ... one *kāyotsarga.*

NOTE.—Saints are not allowed to keep money or to travel in a vehicle of any kind.

For walking along a route teeming with insect life[2] ... ... one *kāyotsarga.*

For travelling over a tract that is full of insect life or at a time when a lot of insects are flying about or floating in the air[2] ... one *kāyotsarga.*

For travelling more than 96 miles in the rainy season for taking part in the accomplishment of some big purpose connected with the *deva* (*Tirthamkara* or the Image of a *Tirthamkara*) or the community of saints, or for a minor celebration in winter or summer[3] ... any penance in the discretion of the leader.

NOTE.—No penance is merited if a saint travel up to 96 miles with the above purpose.[3]

For overstaying beyond a month at a place without a just cause[4] ... ... one *laghumāsa.*

For overstaying for the whole of the rainy season[5] ... ... one *gurumāsa.*

For walking with dusty feet into water[6] one *purumandala.*

For placing wet feet on (a heap of) dust[6] one *purumandala.*

For walking with muddy feet into water[6] one *kalyānaka.*

For crossing over, when walking, a heap of mud or clay, green grass, a ditch, a sheet of water, or insect life, if it be possible to avoid doing so[7] ... one *kalyānaka.*

[1] Ś. 205. [2] Ś. 206-207. [3] Ś. 57. [4] Ś 58. [5] Ś. 58. [6] Ś. 32. [7] Ś. 66.

NOTE.—There is no penalty if it be impossible to avoid doing so.[1]

7—CONCERNING THE SECOND (SWEET SPEECH) SAMITI.

For harsh (or unbecoming) speech[2] ... The vow of silence (for varying lengths of time, according to the seriousness of the offence).

For teaching or encouraging men in the pursuit of occupations which tend to lead to the injury of living beings[2] ... An *upavāsa* or whatever other penance the *āchārya* may deem proper in each case.

8—CONCERNING THE THIRD SAMITI.

For eating objectionable roots, fresh whole fruits, seeds, cereals, pulses or vegetables according to the following table[3]:

Why eaten	Once	Repeatedly
1 Through ignorance	One *kāyotsarga*	One *upavāsa*
2 As a medicine	One *upavāsa*	One *kalyānaka*
3 Without excuse	One *pancha kalyānaka*	*Mūla*

[1] Ch. 66. [2] Ch. 45. [3] Ch. 53.

Offence	Penance
For spitting or uttering sounds or words prior to eating and for not standing properly when eating—	
(*a*) if unwell or unable to stand up properly[1]	one *upavāsa*.
(*b*) otherwise[1]	one *ṣaṣṭha*.
For eating after the occurrence of an *antarāya*[2]	one *upavāsa*.
For eating what has been given up—	
(*a*) if recollection come in the middle of the process of eating[2] ...	desisting from eating, *i.e.*, eating no more of it;
(*b*) if afterwards[2]	one *upavāsa*.
For the occurrence of a serious kind of *antarāya*, *e.g.*, the eating of food contaminated with the presence of things like bone, flesh, etc.	
(*a*) where the knowledge is acquired after eating	one fast + *pratikramaṇa*;
(*b*) where the unclean thing is perceived in one's own hand ..	one *ṣaṣṭha* + *pratikramaṇa*;
(*c*) where the unclean thing has actually got into one's mouth[3]...	a 3 days' fast + *pratikramaṇa*.
For eating, when unwell, food tainted with the *adhākarma* fault, that is, food the preparation of which has involved the destruction of the six kinds of living beings –	
(*a*) if only once	one *upavāsa*;
(*b*) if repeatedly[4]	one *ṣaṣṭha*.

[1] Ch. 54. [2] Ch. 55. [3] Ch. 56. [4] Ch. 57.

For eating, when not unwell, food tainted with the *adhākarma* fault, that is, food the preparation of which has involved the destruction of the six kinds of living-beings –

(*a*) if only once ... ... one *pancha kalyānaka*;
(*b*) if repeatedly ... ... *mūla*.

For eating food contaminated with the *uddiṣṭa* or other faults, in order to keep up study[1] ... ... *niyama* (recitation of the salutation *mantram* nine times).

NOTE.—There are 46 faults which are to be avoided by the saint. He cannot take any food that is tainted with any of them. The *uddiṣṭa* fault occurs when the food is prepared especially for the saint's use.

For going to one village for the daily ramble and to another for food[2] ... *pratikramaṇa* and an *upavāsa*.

For going to a village during the study-time[2] ... ... *kāyotsarga*;
but if for food[2] ... ... one *upavāsa*.

For eating food, through ignorance, at the place of a person of no family or tribe (*varṇa* and caste), *e.g.*, a prostitute

(*a*) if only once and unseen by any one ... ... *pratikramaṇa* and one *upavāsa*;
(*b*) when done repeatedly but unseen by others ... ... one *pancha kalyānaka*;
(*c*) repeatedly when seen by others[3] *mūla*.

For objecting to another's accepting unobjectionable food, through mistake[4] ... one *upavāsa*.

[1] Ch. 58. [2] Ch. 59. [3] Ch. 93-94. [4] Ch. 95.

For objecting to another's accepting unobjectionable food, through personal motive or spite[1] ... ... *pratikramaṇa* and one *pancha kalyānaka*.

For objecting to the gift of unobjectionable books, medicine, the offer of a nightly dwelling, and the like[2] ... one *pancha kalyānaka*.

For refusing, without an adequate cause, to take distasteful or unpalatable food (prepared with things like oil, unsavoury rice, etc.)[3] ... ... *ālochanā*, *kāyotsarga* and an *upavāsa*.

For approving of nursing and assisting in the feeding of sick saints; for keeping, washing, and packing up, etc., the articles that are useful in nursing sick saints, and for bringing approved kind of food for a sick saint, when done for a whole week[4] ... ... *pratikramaṇa*.

For eating and sleeping at one's pleasure (after 3 faults)[5] ... ... *mūla*.

For eating or drinking out of the pots and pans of *Śudras* at whose place the men of the higher castes do not take a meal[6] ... ... five fasts.

NOTE.—There are two kinds of *Śudras* (Kārūs), the *bhojya* and the *abhojya*. Among the former of these are included all those classes of the *Śudra* community at whose place men of the other three castes can dine; the latter are those at whose place no one of the higher classes will dine.[7]

For eating such permissible things as mangoes, *karondas* (*corinda; carissa*

[1] Ch. 95. [2] Ch. 96. [3] Ch. 97. [4] Ch. 98. [5] Ch. 99.
[6] Ch. 151. [7] Ch. 154.

carandus), *vilva khanda*, i.e., *bel* (wood apple), lemon (or citron), when not unwell, separately from the daily meal[1] ...	one *kalyānaka*.
For taking such savoury spices as cloves, cardamums and betel-nut, when not unwell[2]	one *pancha kalyānaka*.
For the use of the quintette of *aṇḍaja* (what is produced from eggs), *vauṇḍaja* (buds), *vālaja* (tendrils), *valkalaja* (bark of trees) and *śṛingaja* (tree-tops)[3]	one *kalyānaka*.
For the use of *śāli*, *brihi*, *kodrava*, *kangu* and *ravaka* (different kinds of small rice)[3]	five *nirvikṛitis*.
For eating at night one kind of food only out of four (substantial things, liquids, semi-liquids and savouries) under stress of illness or fasting[3]	one fast.
For eating at night all kinds of foods under stress of illness or fasting[4] ...	one 2 days' fast.
For any of the ten *śankita* (implying a suspicion of impurity) type of faults in connection with eating[5] ...	one *kalyānaka*.
For the *dāyaka* (where the giver is unclean) fault[5]	one *purumandala*.
For the *miśra* and the *aparinata* faults[5]	one *bhinnamāsa*.

NOTE.—The *miśra* fault signifies the indiscriminate feeding of saints and doubtful saints or laity; the *apariṇata* is the use of water that has not been purified.

For taking food after causing destruction by crushing of—	
(*a*) one-souled type of vegetable life[6]	one *purumandala*;
(*b*) multi-souled " " " "[6]	one *āchāmla*;
(*c*) insect life[6]	one *ekasthāna*.

[1] Ś. 46. [2] Ś. 47. [3] Ś. 50. [4] Ch. 33. [5] Ś. 84. [6] Ś. 88.

For eating while thieves are being beaten in one's sight or 'hearing'—

(*a*) if unwell[1] ... ... one *kalyānaka*;

(*b*) if not unwell[1] ... ... one *bhinnamāsa*.

For taking food after seeing dead bodies of thieves (criminals) killed—

(*a*) if unwell[1] ... ... self-censure;

(*b*) if not unwell[1] .. ... one *kalyānaka*.

For eating at night under external stress[2] .. .. one *pancha kalyānaka*.

For chewing the betel leaf and partaking of what has been given up under external stress[3] ... ... one *kalyānaka*.

For eating beyond measure[4] ... one *kalyānaka*.

For taking food tainted with *himsā* (*i.e.*, the preparation of which has involved injury to the insects or other forms of life)[5] ... ... four *gurumāsas*.

For eating highly rich food[5] ... four *gurumāsas*.

NOTE.—In the last two cases above-mentioned the fault is deemed to have been confessed before the end of a month.[6]

For sitting down, through illness, when eating, or for eating more than once a day—

(*a*) for one fault ... .. one *kalyānaka*;

(*b*) for repeated faults[7] ... ... one *pancha kalyānaka*.

For sitting down, when eating, if done through conceit or boastfulness—

(*a*) for only one fault ... ... *chheda*;

(*b*) for repeated faults[7] ... ... *mūla*.

[1] Ś. 91. [2] Ś. 116. [3] Ś. 115. [4] Ś. 125. [5] Ś. 222. [6] Ś. 222. [7] Ch. 70.

For disregarding a doubt relating to the *udgama*[1] or the *utpādana*[2] faults in connection with the food—
- (*a*) if more than one month has elapsed since ... ... one *kalyānaka*;
- (*b*) after more than four months[3] ... one *pancha kalyānaka*.

For taking such things as *āmlā* (hog plum), *haṛa* (a kind of myrobalan), *baheṛā* (another kind of myrobalan), when not unwell[4] ... ... one *kalyānaka*.

For taking things like mangoes, tamarind, *karondās* (*corinda*; *carissa carundus*), *vilvakhanda*, that is, *bela* (wood apple), lemon (or citron), apart from the meal, and when not unwell[4] one *kalyānaka*.

For excessive fondness for the *rasas* (milk, *ghee*, curds, oil, sugar and salt)[5] one *kalyānaka*.

For carelessly allowing a drop of water to get into the mouth when washing the face[6] ... ... *pratikramaṇa*, a *kāyotsarga*, *ālochanā* and an *upavāsa*.

NOTE.—For the discovery of objectionable elements in food see *Viveka*.

9—CONCERNING THE FOURTH SAMITI (HANDLING THINGS)

For displacing, or carrying from one place to another, stones, wood, straw, tiles and the like[7] .. ... one *kāyotsarga*.

[1] The *udgama* faults refer to the giver and to the manner of preparation of the food.

[2] The *utpādana* faults are those which are concerned with the manner of obtaining food.

[3] Ś. 83. [4] Ś. 46. [5] Ś. 72. [6] Ch. 89. [7] Ch. 61.

For displacing, or carrying from one place to another, stones, wood, straw, tiles and the like, when done during the night (darkness)[1] ... ... one *upavāsa*.

For handling things without examining them, that is, for handling un-examined articles[2] ... ... one *kalyānaka*.

10—Concerning the fifth (Partiṣṭhāpanā) Samiti

For discharging the bodily products (urine, fæces, phlegm, etc.) in un-examined places[2] ... ... one *kalyānaka*.

For discharging the bodily products on growing vegetation, or things endowed with life, or on specifically marked spots, *e.g.*, a platform—

(*a*) if done but once .. ... one *kāyotsarga*;

(*b*) if done repeatedly[3] ... ... one *upavāsa*.

For throwing fæces, urine, etc., in places not intended for the purpose, or in forbidden places[4]... ... . *ratikramaṇa*.

For discharging the functions of nature during the day or at night in un-examined spots[5] ... . one *kāyotsarga*.

[1] Ch. 61. [2] Ś. 213. [3] Ch. 62. [4] Ś. 48. [5] Ś. 207.

11—Concerning the Control of the Senses and Bodily Disregard

For failure to control the senses according to the following table[1] :—

Serial No.	Degree of advancement.	Touch.	Taste.	Smell.	Sight.	Hearing.
1	*Pramatta* (non-vigilant).	1 fast	2 fasts	3 fasts	4 fasts	5 fasts
2	*Apramatta* (vigilant).	1 kāyotsarga.	2 kāyotsargas.	3 kāyotsargas.	4 kāyotsargas.	5 kāyotsargas.

For rubbing the bodily surface to relieve itching or for stretching or contracting the limbs, or jumping and twisting and turning the body[2] ... ... one *kalyānaka*.

For entertaining evil thoughts or desires for the gratification of the senses[3] ... one *kāyotsarga*.

For rubbing (cleaning) the teeth, sleeping on a regular bed (such as is used by laymen) or bathing—

(*a*) if done but once ... ... one *kalyānaka*;

(*b*) if done repeatedly[4] ... ... one *pancha kalyānaka*.

For bathing before women or people of other faiths ... ... one *upavāsa*.

For bathing before women or people of other faiths with soap, oil and the like ... ... one *kalyānaka*.

For decorating the body[5] ... ... one *pancha kalyānaka*.

NOTE.—No penance is necessary for bathing in case of illness[6] or contamination.

[1] Ch. 68. [2] Ś. 213. [3] Ch. 85. [4] Ch. 69. [5] Ś. 99.

For using unguents and pastes under external compulsion[1] ... .. one *kalyānaka*.

For feeling pleased with oneself or with one's luck to be able to obtain the best of the *rasas* (milk, sugar, *ghee*, etc.); for being filled with pride at the lack of want of such things; for 'feeding' the senses; and for the emission of semen, on account of excessive sexual craving[2] ... ... one *pancha kalyānaka*.

For chewing the betel-leaf, using unguents and pastes, and partaking of what has been given up, under external stress[3] ... ... one *kalyānaka*.

NOTE.—External stress includes any kind of trouble or fear of violence, whether caused by friend or foe.

For entertaining a mental craving for the use of such things as air, sunshine, cold[4] ... ... in the discretion of the *āchārya*.

NOTE.—There is ordinarily no penalty for the enjoyment of the things named above; what is objectionable is the entertainment of desire with regard to them.*

For smelling only once[5]

(*a*) an ordinary scent ... ... one *purumandala*;

(*b*) a flower ... ... one *purumandala*.

For smelling more than once, *i.e.* for repeated transgressions in this regard[5]... one *kalyānaka*.

For smelling what has been given up in particular[5] ... ... one *kalyānaka*.

For massaging the limbs and rubbing oil on the body[6] (except when unwell) ... one *kalyānaka*.

[1] Ś. 115. [2] Ś. 114. [3] Ś. 115. [4] Ś. 72. [5] Ś. 71. [6] Ś. 73.

For putting on shoes, or using an umbrella whether made of leaves (straw) or not[1] ... ... one *kalyānaka*.

12—Concerning the Six-Fold Daily Duties

For neglecting to perform or to observe the hours of the *vandanā* (salutation or adoration) and the *pratikramaṇa* duties[2] ... ... one *upavāsa*.

For neglecting the study of the scripture or for not observing the hours fixed for the same[2] ... ... a *kāyotsarga*.

NOTE.—The proper time for 'study' is as follows :—

(*a*) in the morning, from three *gharees* after sunrise;

(*b*) in the afternoon, till three *gharees* before sunset;

(*c*) in the evening from three *gharees* (a *gharee* = 24 minutes) after sunset; and

(*d*) in the night till three *gharees* before sunrise.[2]

The time for adoration is the evening; and that for the day time *pratikramaṇa* ends when half the disk of the sun has sunk below the horizon; the night time self-censure ends with the dawn.[2]

For unnoticed errors in the observance of the daily duties—

(*a*) at the end of a month ... one fast;
(*b*) or at the end of four months ... four fasts;
(*c*) or at the end of eight months ... eight fasts;
(*d*) or at the end of a year[2] ... twelve fasts.

[1] Ś. 75. [2] Ch. 64.

For neglecting the fortnightly and the monthly duties (observances)[1] ...	*pratikramaṇa*+2 fasts.
For neglecting the 4-monthly duty[1] ...	*pratikramaṇa* + eight fasts.
For neglecting the yearly duty[1] ...	*pratikramaṇa*+twenty-four fasts.
For showing disrespect to the six daily duties (after three warnings)[2] ...	*mūla*.
For not observing the rule as to 'study' (*swādhyāya*), self-examination, adoration and the like, or for encouraging others in its disregard[3]	*pratikramaṇa* and one *ṣaṣṭha*.
For omitting to perform, through illness or pain, *vandanā* (adoration), *pratikramaṇa* (self-examination), and *kāyotsarga* for a whole month[4] ...	one *laghu māsa*.
If the above happen through pride[4] ...	one *guru māsa*.
For not doing any of the daily duties under the above circumstances[4] ...	one *laghu chaturmāsa*.
For not doing any of the daily duties without being ill[4]	one *guru chaturmāsa*.
For neglecting to perform the six daily duties (*samāyika*, adoration, reverence of the *Deva* and the like)[5] ...	from one *laghu māsa*[5] to *mūla*.[6]
For not observing the rule of *swādhyāya* (scriptural study) four times a day[5] ...	one *laghu māsa*.
For omitting only one of the six daily duties, or for neglecting to examine the plank, the Books, the whisk or the gourd[5]	one *kalyāṇaka*.

[1] Ch. 66. [2] Ch. 99. [3] Ch. 86. [4] Ś. 221. [5] Ś. 117. [6] Ś. 237.

For forgetting but once *vandanā* and *kāyotsarga* (two of the six parts of *samāyika*)[1] ... ... one *purumandala*.

For forgetting them twice[1] ... ... one *āchāmla*.

For forgetting them three times[1] ... one *upavāsa*.

For concluding the *samāyika* before one's Leader (*āchārya*) if this happen—

(*a*) once ... ... one *purumandala*;
(*b*) twice ... ... one *āchāmla*;
(*c*) thrice[2] ... ... one *upavāsa*.

For not concluding the *kāyotsarga* (the last limb of *samāyika*) with the Leader (that is, for lagging behind)[3]

(*a*) if it occur but once ... one *purumandala*;
(*b*) if it occur twice .. ... one *āchāmla*;
(*c*) if it occur three times[3] ... one *ekasthāna*.

13—Concerning the Keśa Locha

For neglecting, through illness, to perform *keśa locha* for a period of four months ... ... one *upavāsa*.

For neglecting through illness, to perform *keśa locha* for a whole year .. one *ṣaṣṭha*.

For neglecting, through illness, to perform *keśa locha* for five years (one *yuga*)[4] ... ... one *pancha kalyānaka*.

For neglecting to perform *keśa locha* when not unwell[4] ... ... one continuous *pancha kalyānaka*.

For inability to bear the pain of pulling out the hair[5] (*keśa locha*) ... one *kāyotsarga*.

[1] Ś. 118. [2] Ś. 119. [3] Ś. 120. [4] Ch. 67. [5] Ś. 207.

14—Concerning the Renunciation of Clothes

For putting on (resuming) clothes—

(*a*) under persecution ... ... from one *upavāsa*[1] to one *pancha kalyānaka*[2];

(*b*) owing to ill-health ... ... one *ṣaṣṭha*;

(*c*) led by pride or boastfulness ... one *pancha kalyānaka*;

(*d*) in the worst cases (*e g.*, for want of faith)[1] ... ... *mūla*.

15—Concerning Mūla Guṇas

For the transgressions of any of the following 13 *mūla guṇas* (root virtues), namely, 5 *samitis*, 5 sense-controls, *keśa-locha*, sleeping on the ground and the vow against rubbing the teeth[3]

(*a*) if only one fault ... ... one *kāyotsarga*;

(*b*) when committed repeatedly ... one *upavāsa*.

For the transgressions of the remaining 15 *mūla guṇas*, namely, 5 unqualified vows, 6 daily observances, remaining unclothed, non-bathing, standing up while eating and eating only once a day[3]

(*a*) in case of only one fault ... *pratikramaṇa* + one fast;

(*b*) when committed repeatedly ... re-ordination.

NOTE.—Transgressions of vows and of the rules of saintly conduct are of various shades and grades. Their penances also vary with their type and nature, rising in severity with the rise in the sinfulness of the deed. The following table will show a more graduated scale of punishment for various sins.

For violations of the 13 minor *mūla guṇas*[3]

[1] Ch. 68. [2] Ś. 115. [3] Ch. 71.

(*a*) when violated but once[1]

(*i*) for the mildest form of violation	... *mithyākara* (disclaimer);
(*ii*) somewhat less mild	... regret;
(*iii*) in a still more objectionable case ...	... self-censure;
(*iv*) where of a serious type	... confession;
(*v*) more serious than the last	... minor *kāyotsarga* (=recitation of the salutation *mantram* nine times);
(*vi*) if still more serious	... more prolonged *kāyotsarga* (9 to 108 recitations of the salutation *mantram*);
(*vii*) in the worst case	... one full *kāyotsarga* (108 recitations of the *mantram*);

(*b*) when repeatedly violated[1]

(*i*) for a mild form of violation ...	one *purumandala*;
(*ii*) less mild ...	... one *nirvikṛiti*;
(*iii*) in a serious case ...	... one *ekasthāna*;
(*iv*) more serious still ...	... one *āchāmla*;
(*v*) in the worst case ...	... *pratikramaṇa* and an *upavāsa*.

For violations of the remaining 15 *mūla guṇas*[1]

(*a*) when committed but once

(*i*) for the mildest form	... *pratikramaṇa* and an *upavāsa*;
(*ii*) for more serious cases	... more severe *tapa* (according to the type of sinful mentality);

[1] Ch 71.

(b) when repeatedly committed	...	one *ṣaṣṭha*, a 3 days' fast, a 5-days' fast, a fortnight's fast, a month's or six months' or a year's fast; in the worst case, *chheda* (for varying periods), and finally *mūla* (re-ordination).

16—Concerning Uttara Guṇas

The *uttara guṇas* are additional or special accomplishments, over and above the root virtues whose number is eight and twenty. They are either special forms of fastings or of *yoga* austerities. The transgressions of some of them are given here with the proper penances.

For the discontinuance, owing to illness, insect-bite and the like[1] of

(i) the *vriksha mūla*[2] or the *atoraṇa*[3] austerities	...	as many fasts as the number of the days that remained to be completed in the undertaking;
(ii) the *abhrāvakāśa*,[4] the *sthāna*,[5] the *mauna*[6] and		

[1] Ch. 73-74.

[2] The *vriksha mūla* is a form of austerity in which the saint undertakes to stay under a particular tree for a fixed period of time.

[3] The *atoraṇa* is an engagement to stay in the open.

[4] The *abhrāvakāśa* means staying in but not under shade.

[5] The *sthāna* is the vow to remain in one place only.

[6] The *mauna* is the vow of silence.

the *veerāsana*[1] ...	... *ālochanā* and may be *pratikramaṇa* with one day's fast; or any other form of *tapa* penance up to a *pancha kalyānaka*.
For discontinuing, owing to political upheaval, an epidemic, and the like, a *yoga* undertaking with a long fixed period—	
(*i*) if discontinued at the commencement of a fortnight ...	*pratikramṇa* and a *pancha kalyānaka*;
(*ii*) if in the middle of a fortnight	as many fasts as the number of the remaining days in the fortnight;
(*iii*) if at the end of a fortnight[2] ..	one *laghu māsa*.

NOTE.—The disturbed yogas, *sthāna*, *mauna*, etc., should also be re-established.[2]

17—CONCERNING THE BASTIKĀ

For abiding, through ignorance, in a place full of moving or un-moving living beings—[3]	
(*a*) for one fault	one fast;
(*b*) for repeated faults	one *kalyānaka*.

[1] The *veerāsana* is a sitting *yoga* posture, with the right leg doubled under itself at the knee, and the left foot resting on the right thigh. All the above *yoga* forms are undertaken for a fixed period of time, but they admit of one's getting up to discharge the functions of nature. Of the above the *vriksha mūla* and the *atoraṇa* are termed *sthira* (unmoving) and the rest *chala* (moving) *yogas*. According to some *āchāryas* all the *yogas* are *sthira* (unmoving) *yogas*. Two other names of *yogas*, the *ātāpana* and the *avagraha* are mentioned in the text. The *ātāpana* signifies staying in the sun, but the purport of the other has not been ascertained. The penance for the discontinuance of the *avagraha* austerity is the same as that for the *sthāna* and the *mauna* to whose class it belongs; but the penance for the *ātāpana* is not given. It is, however, described as both *sthira* and *chala*.

[2] Ch. 72-74. [3] Ch. 75.

For abiding, through ignorance, in a place full of moving or un-moving living beings when done knowingly —

(*a*) for one fault ... ... *pratikramaṇa* + one *pancha kalyānaka*;

(*b*) for repeated faults[1] ... .. *mūla* (re-ordination).

For exhorting others to build a tower, a village, houses, habitations and the like—

(*a*) when done through ignorance one *kalyānaka*;

(*b*) when done knowingly ... one *pancha kalyānaka*;

(*c*) when done knowingly and boastfully[2] ... ... *mūla* (re-ordination).

For carelessly leaving the door of the dwelling open when leaving ... one *purumandala*;

(*a*) but if a cat or a mongoose or a snake get in ... ... one *upavāsa*;

(*b*) if a thief walk in or rats are killed[3] ... . one *laghu māsa*.

N.B.—If a *bastikā* is found to be objectionable it should be given up at once[4] ... ... *viveka*.

For the disregard of a doubt that arose in connection with the bed or food or *bastikā*, relating to the *udgama* and *utpādana* faults—

(*a*) if more than a month has elapsed[5] since ... ... one *kalyānaka*;

(*b*) where four months have elapsed since[6] ... ... one *pancha kalyānaka*.

NOTE.—The *udguma* faults whose number is sixteen are concerned with the giver and the manner of preparing or making of food or a dwelling place; the *utpādana*, also sixteen in number, have reference to the manner of obtaining either of them (see the Sannyāsa Dharma, Chap. VI).

[1] Ch. 75. [2] Ch. 76. [3] Ś. 90. [4] Ś. 197. [5] Ś. 83.

For carelessly plastering the dwelling place if the floor has become uneven due to rains—

(i) if done on a small scale ... one *purumandala*;

(ii) when done on a large scale[1] ... one *kalyānaka*.

NOTE.—No penance is necessary if the work is done carefully with due care.

For plastering, without due care, the habitation after the performance of the functions of nature[2] ... ... one *purumandala*.

NOTE.—There is no penalty when the plastering is done with due care.

For plastering on a large scale and without due care[3] ... . one *kalyānaka*.

For carelessly plastering the place before or after the natural function[3] ... One *pancha kalyānaka*.

NOTE.—No penalty is incurred if plastering be done with due care, though it may be on a large scale, in the above cases.

For entering a dwelling occupied by other people, or without ascertaining whether it is occupied by the faithful laity or not[4] ... ... one *kalyānaka*.

For causing a disturbance over the use of a proper and properly offered nightly dwelling[5] ... . one *pancha kalyānaka*.

For driving away cattle (that is, preventing them for coming into one's place) in the rain[6] ... ... one *kalyānaka*.

NOTE.—No penalty is incurred by stopping the cattle in any other season.

For not intervening if a thief break into the place—[6]

(a) where no property is lost ... one *kalyānaka*.

(b) where property is stolen .. one *pancha kalyānaka*.

NOTE.—No penance is incurred if the saint utter words of alarm—fire, thief, and the like.[6]

[1] Ś. 85. [2] Ś. 86. [3] Ś. 87. [4] Ś. 125. [5] S. 127. [6] Ś. 103-104.

18—Concerning the Bed and Plank

For not examining the plank and sleeping on it, if the place be free from insects[1]
(a) in the case of a vigilant saint ... a *kāyotsarga*;
(b) in that of a non-vigilant one ... an *upavāsa*;
but if the place be full of insect-life then
for (a) ... ... an *upavāsa*;
and for (b)[1] ... ... one *kalyānaka*.

For the accidental destruction of insect-life during the night, when the plank (bed) had been carefully examined in the day time and the saint had observed all the rules of carefulness when lying down[2] ... a *kāyotsarga*.

For the destruction of a five-sensed form of life on the bed (plank)
(a) if all due carefulness was observed 5 *nirvikṛitis*;
(b) if due care was not taken[3] ... one *kalyānaka*.

For closing and opening doors, whether made of straw or wood, when done for four months in the rainy season[4] ... ... *pratikramaṇa* and an *upavāsa*.

For the disregard of a doubt relating to the purity of the 'bed' ... ... an *upavāsa*;
(a) if more than a month has elapsed since its entertainment ... one *kalyānaka*;
(b) if more than four months have elapsed since[5] ... ... one *pancha kalyānaka*.

Note.—The reference is here to the faults known as the *udgama* and *utpādana* ones, for an explanation of which see under *bastikā ante*.

For sleeping on a cot when in good health[6] one *kalyānaka*.
For the use of a pillow and for covering up the head or the chest with the feather whisk (except when unwell)[6] ... ... one *kalyānaka*.

[1] Ch. 83. [2] S. 204. [3] S. 37. [4] Ch. 87.
[5] S. 83. [6] S. 74.

For using any of the 5 kinds of straws: *śāli, brihi, kodrava, kangu* and *ravaka* (which are different kinds of small rice)[1] ... 5 *nirvikṛitis.*

19—Concerning Sleeping

For repeatedly going to sleep with laymen at a public *dharmaśālā* (hostel or inn), or in a place which is wet or close to the water or where fire is burning[2] ... in the discretion of the leader.

Note.—There is no penance for only one act of this kind.

For sleeping during the day. ... ...

(a) if accustomed to do so before being ordained ... ... one *kalyānaka*;

(b) when not so accustomed[3] ... one *bhinna māsa.*

For falling asleep, during the first watch of the night, without pursuing the Scriptural study, when there is no objection to doing so, on the ground of wind or rain, etc.[4] ... ... one *kalyānaka.*

For the above when the time is not proper for the Scriptural study[4] ... ... one *purumandala.*

20—Concerning Play and Idle Occupations

For playing at a game, out of conceit, though only on being accused of the ignorance thereof[5] ... ... one *pancha kalyānaka.*

For making figures in sand in a spirit of play, for playing charades, for the narration of tales of love, adventure, high life and politics, for acrostics, for repartee in poetry, for making puzzles with straw-nooses[6] ... ... one *purumandala.*

[1] S. 50. [2] S. 56. [3] S. 77. [4] S. 76.
[5] S. 59. [6] S. 60.

For boasting of one's own merit as a composer of poetry, playing at the tug of war or with a ball, for beating tattoo or time on the feather whisk or a bodily limb, touching and pressing one another's body, also for indulging in magic and necromancy

(a) when not seen by people of another faith ... ... one *purumandala* ;

(b) when seen by people of another faith[1] ... ... one *kalyānaka.*

For restraining the movements of living beings, men, insects, etc., by magic or otherwise ... ... simple regret.

For ditto when done for a long time[2] ... one *kalyānaka.*

For becoming engaged in the transmutation of metals, or in making unguents and scents, or in causing the disappearance of things[3]

(a) when not seen by outsiders ... one *kalyānaka* ;

(b) when seen by an outsider ... one *pancha kalyānaka.*

For excessive (side-splitting) laughter[4] ... one *kalyānaka.*

NOTE.—There is no penance for smiling or for a mild kind of laughter.

For making clicking sounds with the tongue or lips, for cracking the fingers, for looking mischievously or coquettishly at a person[5]

(a) in the presence of men of other faiths ... ... one *pancha kalyānaka* ;

(b) when not seen by others ... one *purumandala.*

[1] S. 62. [2] S. 95. [3] S. 61. [4] S. 65.
[5] S. 67.

For rubbing the body to relieve itching, for jumping and twisting the body, and for turning it round[1] ... ... one *kalyānaka.*

For thinking evil and entertaining unbecoming thoughts[2] ... ... *pratikramaṇa.*

For stretching and contracting the limbs, needlessly, through uneasiness, caused by the contact of an object or otherwise[2] ... one *purumandala.*

For throwing pebbles[2] ... ... one *kalyānaka.*

For throwing stones[2] ... ... one *pancha kalyānaka.*

For narrating tales of love, adventure, high life and statesmanship (diplomacy)

(i) for one fault ... ... one *purumandala*;

(ii) for repeated faults[3] ... ... one *pancha kalyānaka.*

For becoming absorbed in singing and dancing[3] ... ... self-censure.

For coming out of one's place to enjoy singing or dancing[3] ... ... one *kalyānaka.*

For resort to violence—kicking, hitting, beating, etc.[4] ... ... *pratikramaṇa.*

For encouraging men to create a disturbance by singing and dancing[5] ... a 3-days' fast.

For collecting material that is not devoid of life, with a view to ascertain whether certain supernatural powers have been acquired or not[6] ... ... one *laghu māsa.*

NOTE.—There is no penance for collecting selected pure (lifeless) articles in the above circumstances.

For trying the merit of a recipe on a householder [7] ... ... one *pancha kalyānaka.*

1 S. 213. 2 S. 190. 3 S. 70. 4 S. 190.
5 Ch. 51. 6 S. 96. 7 S. 97.

For trying the merit of a recipe on a nun[1] ... one *kalyānaka*.

NOTE.—There is no penalty for trying a medicine on a saint, and probably none on a menstruant nun.

For trying a medicine on small animals, rats, snake and the like[2] ... ... expression of regret.

But if the animals die[2] ... ... one *chaturamāsa*.

21—CONCERNING MISCHIEF AND DESTRUCTION OF THINGS

For destroying things like a needle, a nail-parer, a knife or other metallic article[3] ... As many fasts as the finger-breadths of length in the article destroyed. According to some Leaders the finger-breadths are to be counted in a *ghanāngula* (a cubic finger).

For destroying the plank, the feather-whisk, the gourd, etc., belonging to another saint[3] ... ... a *kāyotsarga*.

For damaging or destroying a painting, paper, canvas, parchment and the like[4] ... a *kāyotsarga*.

For destroying or breaking pieces of thread, straw, wood or wooden fibre with the fingers or the teeth[5] ... ... one *kalyānaka*.

NOTE.—The penalty is greater if the above acts are done at night than when done during the day.[5]

For entertaining evil thoughts and desire[6] for sense-gratification ... ... one *kāyotsarga*.

For entertaining evil or unbecoming thoughts[7] *pratikramaṇa*.

1 S. 97. 2 S. 98. 3 Ch. 84. 4 Ch. 85.
5 S. 215. 6 Ch. 85. 7 S. 190.

For scraping wood and other material things

(1) when done with a small instrument, like a pair of scissors, nail-parer, etc. ... ... one *laghu māsa;*

(2) when done with a big thing like a hunting knife ... ... one *guru māsa;*

(3) when done with an axe or a carpenter's tool ... ... one *laghu chaturmāsa;*

(4) when done with a pick-axe and other large-sized instruments[1] ... one *guru chaturmāsa.*

For becoming engaged in breaking things[2]

(1) when done with one hand ... one *laghu māsa;*

(2) when done with one hand and with the aid of a stone or pestle ... one *guru māsa;*

(3) when done by holding a heavy weight in both hands ... one *laghu chaturmāsa;*

(4) when done by holding a huge pestle like crushing instrument with both hands ... ... one *guru chaturmāsa.*

22—Concerning Worship

For exhorting men, through ignorance, to perform a worship-ceremonial[3]

(a) for one fault ... ... *pratikramaṇa* with *ālochanā*, *kāyotsarga* or an *upavāsa* (according to the scale on which the worship is to be performed).

(b) for repeated faults ... ... one *kalyānaka*

For ditto when done knowingly[4]

(a) for one fault ... ... *pratikramaṇa* and one *kalyānaka*

(b) for repeated faults ... ... one *pancha kalyānaka.*

1 S. 219. 2 S. 220. 3 Ch. 77. 4 Ch. 78.

For ditto where the destruction of living beings of the six classes is involved ... re-ordination (*mūla*).

23—Concerning Respect and Disrespect

For showing respect to, or attending upon, a false saint
  (a) if with a view to learn wisdom from him ... ... mere regret,
  (b) without such a motive[1] ... one *pancha kalyānaka*.

For going forward to meet a nun (to show her respect)[2] ... ... four *guru māsas*.

For saluting the wrongly-directed (men of wrong faiths)[2] ... ... four *guru māsas*.

These faults must be confessed within a month's time; otherwise probably the penalty will be severer.[2]

NOTE.—The Jaina Saints do not salute any one except other Jaina Saints. They do not salute even ordinary Jainas; but they will wish "increase of merit" and the like to all who come to see them or who offer them salutation.

For saluting a lax saint (the *pārśvastha*) and suspending or interrupting the recitation of the Scripture in order to do so, before a great gathering of men[1] ... one *māsika*.

NOTE.—Ordinarily no fault is committed if an *āchārya* or an ordinary saint salute a lax ascetic of the Jaina faith.[3]

No penalty is incurred by a saint if he behave respectfully towards the five kinds of lax saints, the *pārśvastha*, the *kuśila*, the *avasanna*, the *mṛigachāri*, and the *sansakta*, expecting that they will behave respectfully towards him. No fault is committed even, if for a short period of time, he show them respect and join them in the study of the Scripture. If they are not respectful towards him he should part company from them.[4]

1 Ś. 79. 2 Ś. 222.
3 Ś. 109. 4 Ś. 108.

There is no penalty for the following :—

(a) for treating a king, a military commander, a police officer, a minister, a high priest of another faith and the like with respectful esteem to engender love in their hearts for the protection of the community[1] ...

(b) for responding, by standing up, coming forward, offering a seat, appearing pleased, and suffering a smile to appear on one's lips, or speaking sweetly in response to similar marks of esteem from the laity and even men of the other faiths: unless this be done from a motive or to be considered great or from pride in which case the penalty is[2] ... ... one *pancha kalyānaka;*

(c) for standing up to receive a physician when he comes to see a sick person[3] ... ...

(d) for occupying a seat or throne when offered by a king in his audience hall[3] ... ...

(e) for suffering men, whether big or small, to worship one when one remains unaffected by pride: otherwise the penalty is[4] ... ... one *pancha kalyānaka.*

For showing disrespect to or lowering the dignity of the Scripture of Truth and of its significancy[5] ... ... from *ālochanā* and a *kāyotsargaš* to *pāranchika parihāra*[6]

1 S. 110. 2 S. 111. 3 S. 112. 4 S. 113. 5 Ch. 81.
6 S. 249.

For finding fault with the five kinds of divine Preceptors[1]	*pratikramaṇa* and a *kāyotsarga* and an *upavāsa*.
For showing disrespect to the *Tirthamkara*, the Founder of the faith, the Guṇadharas (Apostles of the *Tirthamkaras*), the *ācharya*, and the like[2]	from *pratikramaṇa* to *pāranchika*.[3]
For lowering the teaching of Saints and the Scripture of Truth in the estimation of men[4]	one *upavāsa* (to *pāranchika*).[5]
For not showing, through laziness, that is lack of vigilance, proper courtesy and respect to a brother saint, whether belonging to one's own *gaṇa* or to another, and not holding with him saintly intercourse—greeting, bidding farewell, interchange of ideas, confession of sins, etc.,—which are permissible to a saint[6]	expulsion from the province for one year.
For writing the Scriptural text on ground or stone[7]	an *upavāsa*.
For ditto on one's own stomach or arm[7] ...	*ālochanā*.
For showing disrespect to the great Salutation *mantram*, the six daily duties, the five great vows of Saints, and disregarding the observance known as *asedhikā* and *nisedhikā* (after 3 faults)[8]	*mūla*.
For doing any of the following acts without first obtaining the leave of his Leader (*āchārya*): discharging the functions of nature, going to a village for *charyā* (for rambling or food) or to a hamlet more than a *kosa* (2 miles) distant[9]... ...	one *purumandala*.

1 Ch. 80. 2 S. 190. 3 S. 249. 4 Ch. 82. 5 S. 250. 6 Ch. 90-91. 7 Ch. 92. 8 Ch. 99. 9 S. 124.

For showing disrespect to a brother saint, filled with pride of caste, family, wisdom and the like[1] ... ... one *pancha kalyānaka.*

For not observing[2] the rule of *ichchhākāra*[3] one *purumandala.*

For defiling the true faith[4] ... ... *pāranchika parihāra.*

For not saying "*nisahi, nisahi, nisahi*" when entering and "*asahi, asahi, asahi*" when leaving a temple, a cave or *maṭha* and the like at night

(i) if it occur but once ... ... one *purumandala* ;
(ii) if twice ... ... one *āchāmla* ;
(iii) if three times[5] ... ... one *upavāsa.*

For neglecting the rule of *asedhikā, nisedhikā, mithyākāra, nimantaraṇa* and *ichchhākāra*[6] ... ... one *purumandala.*

NOTE.—*Asedhikā* is the utterance of the formula "*asahi, asahi, asahi*" ; *nisedhikā* is "*nisahi, nisahi, nisahi*" ; *mithyākāra* is "*may my fault be annulled*"; to ask for a permissible accessory of *sannyāsa* (a gourd, a feather whisk, books or the writing materials), with becoming gentility, is *nimantaraṇa*; and *ichchhākāra* is the spirit of respectful acquiescence in the word of the leader (*āchārya*).

24—Concerning Pupils and Castes

For ordaining a small boy, or a very old person[7] ... ... from one *pancha kalyānaka*[8] to 6 *guru māsas.*

For ordaining a man of low caste or the son of a slave girl[7] ... ... 6 *guru māsas.*

For ordaining a pregnant woman or an impotent person[7] ... ... from 6 *guru māsas* to *mūla*[9] ;

For ordaining a *pariah*[10] ... ... *mūla.*

1 S. 68. 2 S. 122. 3 Ichchhākāra is the respectful acquiescence in the word of the *āchārya* (Leader), and veneration for his person. 4 S. 250. 5 S. 121. 6 S. 122. 7 S. 223. 8 S. 127. 9 S. 237. 10 S. 241.

For going into another *gachcha* (community) of saints than one's own, that is, the one in which one was ordained[1]	*chheda* of half of one's seniority.

NOTE.—If the *mūla* has been incurred by the *āchārya* himself in this connection, he will nevertheless observe only some form of fasting instead of it.[2]

For ordaining a tried and experienced officer of the state at a time when his services are indispensable for the public good[3] ...	*pāranchika parihāra.*
For accepting the duly ordained and well-qualified pupil of another *āchārya* (Leader)[4]	one *pancha kalyānaka.*
For ordaining knowingly a man of no *kula* (family), from conceit of one's *ṛiddhis* (miraculous powers), or from the desire to increase the number of one's pupils, if the pupil is given up[5]	one *pancha kalyānaka.*
For ordaining a man of an untouchable caste under the above circumstances[6] ...	2 *pancha kalyānakas.*
For not dissociating with a pupil of no *kula* (family) when the fact is discovered[7] ...	cessation of intercourse.

NOTE.—No penalty is incurred in case of ignorance, if the pupil be given up. It would appear from *ślokas* 105—108 of the Chulika that Sudras are not allowed to aspire to saintly life; but under *śloka* No. 154 of the same Book those of the Śudras at whose place the men of the three higher *varṇas* may dine or in whose vessels they may drink water (termed *Bhojya kārūs*) may rise as high as the highest step on the householder's path. Whether this distinction is scientific or only social, adopted under stress of persecution or ridicule from the men of the more widely-prevalent caste-ridden rival sect, is not quite clear. The probability is in favour of the latter view, especially as *śloka* 113 of the Chulika would seem to exclude from sainthood all those persons who are not born of parents of the

1 Ch. 104. 2 S. 127. 3 S. 250. 4 Ch. 105.
5 Ch. 105—110 and 113. 6 Ch. 110. 7 Ch. 109.

same *varṇa*, that is those whose parents belong to different (though superior) *varṇas*. According to the commentary to *śloka* No. 98 of the Chulika a saint should not take his food even at the house of a Sūta, that is, a person born of a *Brāhmāṇa* woman by a *Kshatriya* father; but Prince Abhya Kumar, who was the son of King Shrenik from a *Brāhmaṇa rāni*, was not only a very great Jaina of his age, but he also actually attained salvation! The case of the *abhojya* (untouchable) Śudra is, however, different, and rests on entirely different grounds.

NOTE.—A saint is required to bathe with 'pure' water if he happen to touch an untouchable person.[1]

For the abduction of a saint of another faith, or of a layman, a woman, a child, or of the pupil of a brother saint[2] ...	*anupasthāpanā parihāra*.
For accepting food, through ignorance, from the hand of an outcaste *pariah*, and for continuing with one's food after beholding an out-caste *pariah*[3]	*pratikramaṇa* and 2 *pancha kalyānakas*.
For associating with an untouchable *pariah* or for rubbing the body against that of an out-caste *pariah*[3]	one *pancha kalyānaka*.

NOTE.—The mind is not pleased with the appearance of dirt at the time of eating; and the appearance of an embodiment of extreme filth, in the shape of an untouchable *pariah*, is not unlikely to prove very harmful under the influence of "suggestion." The saints, therefore, will discontinue their meal under the circumstances.

25—Concerning Sickness and Nursing

For extinguishing the fire that has been brought to relieve the distress or ailment of another saint	5 *nirvikṛitis*.

1 Ch. 136. 2 S. 245. 3 Ch. 101. 4 S. 42.

For ditto when done under the influence of mild passions[1] ... ... one *kalyānaka*.

For bringing oneself in touch with the flame, that is, warming oneself, while warming a sick brother or heating an utensil for his use[2] ... ... 5 *nirvikṛitis*.

For ditto when done repeatedly[3] ... one *kalyānaka*.

For lighting a fire under the orders of the physician

(i) without consulting the sick saint[4] ... one *pancha kalyānaka*;

(ii) at the desire of the latter

(a) for the lighter of the fire .. one *kalyānaka*.

(b) for the sick saint (on recovery)[4] ... one *pancha kalyānaka*.

For eating more than he should, or for partaking of the objectionable "multi-souled" vegetables, such as onions, when sick[5] ... ... one *kalyānaka*.

For using unclean things, *e.g.*, a bone, even though only once[6] ... ... one *pancha kalyānaka*.

For applying medicine to one's own wound in any other than the rainy season[7] ... one *kalyānaka*.

NOTE.—In the rainy season no penalty is incurred by the saint as the danger of complications is too great then.

For the use of pure (life-less) medicines, with full care,

(i) in case of unbearable suffering ... expression of regret;

(ii) when the pain is not unbearable[8] ... one *kalyānaka*.

For the above (a) where the malady is not unbearable and the medicine is not used with due care[8] ... ... one *pancha kalyānaka*;

1 S. 42. 2 S. 43. 3 S. 44. 4 S. 45.
5 S. 47. 6 S. 51. 7 S. 198. 8 S. 80.

(b) where the medicine is not used with full care, but the malady is unbearable (serious)1 ... ... one *kalyānaka*.

For disregarding a doubt as to the 'purity' of the drugs used[2] ... ... one *ekasthāna*.

For rubbing, crushing or grinding a number of pure (life-less) things[2] ... ... self-censure.

For the above in case the things are endowed with life (fresh or green)[2] ... one *upavāsa*.

For washing pots collected together for nursing sick saints[3]

(i) when their number is very great ... one *ṣaṣṭha*;

(ii) when their number is large ... one *upavāsa*;

(iii) when they are not very many ... one *ekasthāna*;

(iv) when they are only a few ... one *āchāmla*.

For approving of nursing and assisting in the feeding of sick saints, for keeping, washing, packing up, etc., the articles that are useful in nursing sick saints and for bringing approved kind of food for a sick saint, when done for a whole week[4]... *pratikramaṇa*.

For taking a purgative or something to cause vomiting to cure oneself ... *pratikramaṇa* and an *upavāsa*.

For neglecting to nurse and serve a sick saint[6] ... ... *pratikramaṇa*.

NOTE.—There is no penance for taking such medicinal things as *āmlā* (hog plum), *haṛa* (a kind of myrobalan), *baheṛā* (another kind of myrobalan), in illness. Similarly, there is no penalty for taking things like mangoes, tamarind, *karondās* (*corinda; carissa carandus*), *vilvakhanda*, that is, *bel* (wood apple), lemon (or citron) when unwell.[7]

1 Ś. 80. 2 Ś. 82. 3 Ś. 100. 4 Ch. 98. 5 Ch. 100.
6 Ś. 192. 7 Ś. 46.

It would appear from the language of *śloka* 47 that no expiation is incurred if a sick saint take such medicinal and breath-purifying spices as cardamums, cloves and betelnuts.[1] The saint is expressly allowed to use such things as a pin or needle, or an instrument for lifting pots and kettle from the fire.[2] There is also no penalty for the use of a wooden plank or seat, a mat or gourd or a hollow utensil.[3]

No penalty is incurred by entertaining sympathy for a co-religionist, or for serving the owner of the resting place or the giver of food in his sickness, provided living 'matter' is not handled.[4] No penance is likewise required for attending, with due carefulness, on a co-religionist layman, or even on the people of another faith, when sick.[5]

No penance is necessary for putting on clothes, for sleeping on a cot, for massaging the bodily limbs and for applying or rubbing oil on the body, when done to alleviate pain.[6] Similarly, no penalty is incurred by the use of a pillow and the covering up of the head or the chest with the feather-whisk, during illness.[6] If a saint who is unwell put on shoes, or use an umbrella made of leaves to protect his head against the sun, no penance is indicated.[7]

26—Concerning Accessories (*Upakarana*)

The accessories for "sense-control" are of three kinds:

(1) of the most 'valuable,' type—Books

(2) of the middling type—the feather-whisk and the gourd,[8]

(3) of the lower type—writing materials.

The penance for losing them is as follows[9]:—

For losing those of the greatest utility ... one fast.

For those of the middling utility ... one *āchāmla*.

For those of the lower utility ... ... one *purumandala*.

1 S. 47. 2 S. 51. 3 S. 52. 4 S. 106. 5 S. 107.
6 S. 73. 7 S. 75.
8 Some authorities place the gourd in the third class. 9 S. 58.

For suffering, through carelessness, any of the accessories to be destroyed or rendered unserviceable [1] ... ... one *pancha kalyānaka*.

NOTE.—According to another text the penance is only

(1) for the destruction of the accessory of the highest utility ... ... one 2 days' fast;

(2) for one of the middling utility ... one fast;

(3) for one of the lower utility [1] ... one *āchāmla*.

For using things endowed with life (green leaves and the like) in the preparation of a feather-whisk, book, etc.[2] ... ... one *kalyānaka*.

For working unremittingly for the period of four months[2] for the preparation of an accessory ... ... one *kalyānaka*.

Do. by neglecting the scriptural study[2] one *pancha kalyānaka*.

NOTE.—No penance is necessary where the things are pure (lifeless), and none where the work is done in the leisure intervals.

For neglecting the rule of *nimantaraṇa*, that is, making a request for a gourd, a feather-whisk, a book or the writing materials, with becoming meekness [3] ... one *purumandala*.

For not cleaning the gourd after every fortnight[4] one *upavāsa* and *pratikramaṇa*.

NOTE.—The saint is required to clean the gourd once every fortnight, to keep it free from insect-life.

For helping oneself (taking without its being given) [5]

(a) a book or books ... ... one *laghu māsa*;

(b) a feather-whisk ... ... one *kalyānaka*;

(c) a gourd or any other object of the lowest utility, e.g., a writing pen ... one *purumandala*.

1 S. 54. 2 S. 78.
3 S. 122. 4 Ch. 88. 5 S. 123.

28—Concerning Miscellaneous Matters

(a) *Keeping Bad Company*

For keeping the company of men of false religions or walking with those who lead undisciplined lives [1] ... ... *pratikramaṇa*, a *kāyotsarga* and an *upavāsa*.

For being insulted, whether deservedly or undeservedly (Ch. 102) ... ... departure from the place.

For keeping the company of unsaintly saints by one who pulls himself up readily after a slip ... ...

(i) if he return within six months ... *tapa* penance ;

(ii) if after six months [2] ... ... chheda (for the whole length of the period of absence).

(b) *Sallekhanā and Tapa*

For taking food when unable to bear the hardships consequent on the *sallekhanā* vow or on a prolonged fast

(a) when eaten in secret ... ... *pratikramaṇa* and an *upavāsa* ;

(b) if eaten publicly or before another person [3] ... ... one *pancha kalyānaka*;

(c) *Earning a Living*

For obtaining or earning one's livelihood by means of palmistry, phrenometry, medicine, incantations and the like [4] ... *pratikramaṇa* and an *upavāsa*

(d) *Deserting the Sangha*

For falling away from the true saintly path and roaming about in unsaintly or less-saintly styles [5] ... ... chheda for as much

[1] Ch. 80. [2] S. 230. [3] Ch. 79. [4] Ch. 81. [5] S. 228-229.

	time as the transgressor remains away from the true path.

NOTE.—Those who have been admitted in the order by any of the unsaintly or less-saintly saints should be ordained afresh by *mūla*.[1]

For leaving the *sangha* (company of saints) and for moving about alone[2]	chheda for the full period of desertion.
For teaching methods of trades that involve injury to living beings of six[3] kinds, and for encouraging men to embark on them[4]	from one *upavāsa* upwards (in the discretion of the *āchārya*).
For the defilement of conduct (gross lack of discipline) and the violation of the principal vows[5]	*mūla*.
For the (complete) non-observance of the six daily duties[5]	*mūla*.
For propounding doctrines that are opposed to the Teaching of the Jaina Religion[6] ...	*mūla*.
For adopting the life of unsaintly mendicants, and for less-saintly (lax) modes of conduct[7]	*mūla*.
For adopting the mode and style of the *sādhus* of the non-Jaina Faiths[8] ...	*mūla*.
For falling back into the householder's stage[8]	*mūla*.
For insincerity in the adoption of the saint's vows[8]	*mūla*.
For the commission of sins that are destructive of *mūla guṇas* (root virtues)[9] ...	*mūla*.

1 S. 239. 2 S. 227.

3 These are: four kinds of souls whose bodies are made of a single element (earth, water, fire and air), vegetable-life and moving living beings.

4 Ch. 45. 5 S. 237. 6 S. 238.

7 S. 239. 8 S. 240. 9 S. 241.

For the loss of faith[1] ... ... *mūla*.

NOTE.—If a saint loses faith in the Jaina Faith, but reverts to it of his own accord without his change of belief becoming known to any one he may select his own penance (whatever he pleases); but if the matter is known to any one then he should be given the *mūla*.[2]

For joining the king's enemies[3] ... ... *pāranchika parihāra*.

For being an enemy of the reigning king[4] .. *pāranchika parihāra*.

For ordaining an officer of state when his services are most needed in the public interest[4] ... ... *pāranchika parihāra*.

For ravishing or falling in love with the queen[5] *pāranchika parihāra*.

(e) *Exhibiting Fear*

For climbing a tree, deviating into a disused or unused path, throwing stones or pieces of wood, when done through fear[6] one *kalyānaka*.

For closing up the hole of a snake or rat[6] one *kalyānaka*.

NOTE.—No penalty is incurred when the closing up is only temporary, and when the covering is removed in the morning at the time of departure from the place.[6]

For becoming frightened by the appearance or sounds of another (living being) ... expression of regret.

For falling down through fright[7] ... self-censure.

For running away from fear[7] ... ... one *kalyānaka*.

NOTE.—If the above happen when the saint is unwell, there will be no penance.[7]

For running away from rain or fire, and causing others to run[8]

(i) when unwell[3] ... ... self-censure

(ii) when not unwell ... ... one *kalyānaka*.

1 S. 237. 2 S. 253-254. 3 S. 249. 4 S. 251.
5 S. 250. 6 S. 89. 7 S. 92. 8 S. 94.

(iii) for tearing along at top speed under the above circumstances ... one *pancha kalyānaka.*

(f) *Lack of Learning*

For inability to settle the doubts of the congregation when discoursing on the Scripture or on the purport of the language of the Teaching of Truth[1] ... ... an *upavāsa.*

For entering into a debate without being qualified to do so, if it ends disastrously[2] one *kalyānaka.*

NOTE.—There is no penance in the above case if the debate is carried out successfully.[2]

(g) *Forgetting the Nursing Penance (Vaiyāvritya)*

For forgetting *vaiyāvritya* (nursing) penance[3] *pratikramaṇa.*

(h) *Bodily Purification*

For using much water or clay for purification[4] ... ... *pratikramaṇa* and an *upavāsa.*

(i) *Grief*

For feeling sorrowful on forgetting to observe any of the *samitis* (rules of vigilance), or on parting from the four-fold *sangha* (community of saints, nuns, laymen and lay women) or for damage being done to a book or some other thing[5] ... *mithyākara* (annulment or disclaimer of the action).

For abandoning oneself to grief or for weeping, under the above circumstances[5] ... one *kalyānaka.*

(j) *Disclosing Confession and Faults*

For disclosing to another person the faults that have been confessed before the *āchārya*[6] ... ... one *pancha kalyānaka.*

1 Ch. 82. 2 S. 59. 3 S. 102. 4 Ch. 100.
5 S. 81. 6 Ch. 103.

For disclosing the faults of the *chatura-varṇa sangha* (literally the community of 4 castes), that is to say, of the saints, nuns, laymen and lay women of the Jaina community [1] ... ... expulsion.

NOTE.—If the transgressor subsequently, sincerely show repentance for his sin he may be re-admitted into the *sangha* in the presence of the four-fold community.

(k) *Violence and Excitement of Passions*

For ordinary violence, that is kicking, beating, fighting, etc. [2] ... ... instant *pratikramaṇa*.

NOTE.—Severer penance will be needed for really serious cases of undignified unsaintly behaviour.

For assaulting or striking a saint with a stick [3] ... ... *pāranchika parihāra*.

For harsh speech [4] ... ... the vow of silence.

For quarrelling when observed by the people of an other faith [5] ... ... the vow of silence and one or more fasts.

For creating a disturbance by abusive or harsh speech [6] ... ... the vow of silence and 5 fasts.

For creating a disturbance publicly [7] ... *locha* or one or more fasts which may extend to six months or more in the discretion of the Leader.

For assault or causing hurt [8] ... ... one or more fasts.

For inciting others to cause a disturbance by gesture [9] ... ... a number of *gaṭṭhas* which may extend to six months.

NOTE.—No one should speak to such an evil-minded person.

1 Ch. 52. 2 S. 100. 3 S. 245. 4 Ch. 45.
5 Ch. 46. 6 Ch. 47. 7 Ch. 48. 8 Ch. 49. 9 Ch. 50.

For waking up a sleeping vow-less (undisciplined) layman; and for encouraging men create a disturbance by singing and dancing[1]	a 3-days' fast.
For being the cause of the entertainment of angry or painful feelings in the heart of another[2]	*pratikramaṇa*.
For yielding to the sway of passions	
(a) if regretted in the very next moment	no further penance.
(b) if they survive a day and a night (that is, for 24 hours) ...	one *kalyānaka*.
(c) in still more stubborn cases[3] ...	one *pancha kalyānaka*.
For exciting angry or painful feelings in the heart of a person[4]	*pratikramaṇa*.
For failure to apologise after a fault when the transgressor does not leave the *sangha* (community)	
(i) in the case of ordinary saint ...	5 days' *chheda* for every 24 hours' failure;
(ii) for a specially qualified or learned saint	10 days' *chheda* for every 24 hours.
(iii) for an *āchārya*[5]	15 days' for every 24 hours.
For leaving the *sangha* without apologising for a fault	
(i) for an ordinary saint ...	10 days' *chheda* for every 24 hours.

1 Ch. 51. 2 Ś. 193. 3 Ś. 69.
4 Ś. 193. 5 Ś. 231-232.

(ii) in the case of an advanced or specially qualified saint	15 days' *chheda* for every 24 hours.
(iii) in the case of an *āchārya*[1] ...	20 days' *chheda* for every 24 hours.

(l) *Common Happenings and Mishaps*

For the general (unobserved) faults of saintly life after every month	one *upavāsa*;
or after every four months ...	4 fasts;
or after every eight months ...	8 fasts;
or after every year [2]	12 fasts.
For sneezing, yawning and passing wind[3]	*pratikramaṇa*.
For the coming out of a worm from the saint's body[4]	one *kāyotsarga*.
For the death of an insect caused by its coming into violent contact with the body of the saint[4]	one *kāyotsarga*.
For throwing away old accessories (the feather-whisk, gourd and the like) of saintly life[4]	one *kāyotsarga*.
For the faults of commission and omission in connection with the daily study, recitation or discourse, as well as for not observing strictly punctually the time for the same[5]	one *kāyotsarga*.
For going through various daily, nightly, fortnightly, monthly, four-monthly, yearly and death-bed processes of *pratikramaṇa* in a hurry, or for unknown faults committed in their execution[6]	one *kāyotsarga*.

1 Ś. 233. 2 Ch. 65. 3 Ś. 192.
4 Ś. 207. 5 Ś. 208. 6 Ś. 209.

For interruption, through illness, in carrying out the penance given (on recovery)[1] ...	one *kalyānaka*.
For interruption on account of special duty in the service of one's Leader (*āchārya*), in the middle of the penance (on return)[2]	one *kalyānaka*.
For interruption on account of special duty in connection with religion, or the service of the community of the saints (on return from special duty)[3]	one *kalyānaka*.
For faults committed because of the natural imperfections in the performance of austerities and the control of the body and the mind[4]	one *kāyotsarga*.
For the various forms of movements however carefully executed (inasmuch as all movements are opposed to the nature of pure spirit)[5]	one *kāyotsarga*.
For the movements performed with due care whilst away from one's own community[6]	one *kāyotsarga*.
For visiting another party of saints, though all faults are avoided when doing so[7] ...	one *kāyotsarga*.
For repeating a fault in spite of penance[8] ...	a 3 days' fast.

1 S. 216. 2 S. 217. 3 S. 218. 4 S. 185.
5 S. 186-187. 6 S. 188. 7 S. 189. 8 Ch. 51.

SPECIAL RULES APPLICABLE TO NUNS

The nun is entitled generally to all the forms of penance, excepting *sthāpanā* (*parihāra*).[1] She may be required to observe the fasting penances even beyond the usual limit of six months that has been fixed for this age. But in that case the penance would terminate at the end of the seventh month.[1] The nun is also not to be given the *pinchha*, the *chheda* and the *mūla* penances.[1] Nor is she to be given a *dina-pratimā* (a whole day's *kāyotsarga*) or the *trai-kāla yoga* (*kāyotsarga* for the three periods, namely, morning, noon and evening).[2]

The special penalties applicable to her case are given below.

For washing, or cleaning, the clean as well as unclean utensils[3] ... ... one *pancha kalyānaka*.

NOTE.—No penance is required to be undergone when the nun only washes those utensils that are used in *vaiyāvrita* (attending on sick saints).[3]

For washing the pots separately, to make them look neat, whether they be clean or unclean[4] ... ... one *pancha kalyānaka*.

For washing pots and pans not besmeared with food, along with those so besmeared[5] one *pancha kalyānaka*.

1 Ś. 158. 2 Ch. 114. 3 Ś. 102.
4 Ś. 101. 5 Ś. 102.

For cleaning (rubbing) the teeth, by deliberately disregarding the Scriptural injunction to the contrary [1]	avoidance of *rasas* milk, curd, *ghee*, oil, sugar and salt) for a period of six months.
For violating the vow of chastity [2] ...	expulsion.
For giving gold, silver, etc. (of which she might be secretly possessed) to her relatives [3]	*pratikramaṇa* and a *ṣaṣṭha*.
For possessing property [4]	giving it away for the well-being of living beings
For the uncleanness of the menses [5] ...	living on rice from which water has been drained off, or on *n i r a s a* (*rasa*-less) food, or going without it altogether.

NOTE.—The nun performs the six daily duties in silence during the menses, and afterwards goes to the Leader (*āchārya*) to take some expiation from him for the uncleanness.[6]

For visiting people's houses without a reason; for weeping, bathing, or feeding children, cooking, engaging herself in the householders' occupations [7]	
(1) if she be of a wavering disposition	
(a) and the fault be committed through negligence	
(i) for one fault	one *ṣaṣṭha*;
(ii) for repeated faults	one *kalyāṇaka*;

1 Ch. 123. 2 Ch. 124. 3 Ch. 130. 4 Ch. 131.
5 Ch. 134. 6 Ch. 135. 7 Ch. 115-116.

(b) if the fault is committed deliberately
  (i) for one fault ... ... one *ṣaṣṭha* ;
  (ii) for repeated faults ... ... one *pancha kalyānaka;*

(2) if she be unwavering
  (a) and the fault is committed through negligence
    (i) for one fault ... ... one *kāyotsarga;*
    (ii) for repeated faults ... ... one *upavāsa;*
  (b) if the fault is committed deliberately
    (i) for one fault ... ... one *upavāsa* ;
    (ii) for repeated faults ... ... one *kalyānaka* ;

For plastering (a wall or floor), washing medicine-pots, lighting a fire, and the like[1] from one *kāyotsarga* to one *pancha kalyānaka* (according to the scale involved).

For washing clothes[2] ... ... one *upavāsa*.

For washing the plate and saucer used in eating[2] ... ... one *kāyotsarga*.

For keeping a third piece of cloth, besides the two allowed[3] ... ... one *pancha kalyānaka*.

NOTE.—Nuns are to accept (whether asked for or not) two pieces of cloth to cover their upper and lower limbs, and a bowl in which they are to fetch food from the place of a layman.[4]

For sleeping, walking, or going in the company of a young saint (for a young nun), and for performing *kāyotsarga* with him[5] thirty fasts.

NOTE.—A woman is considered youthful up to the age of sixty years.[6] This is from the point of view of propriety, and the observance of the rule of celibacy. But it is not objectionable for a nun to live with and walk, etc., in the company of her own father and brother.[6]

1 Ch. 117. 2 Ch. 118. 3 Ch. 119. 4 Ch. 120.
5 Ch. 121. 6 Ch. 122.

SPECIAL RULES FOR HOUSEHOLDERS

The householders (laymen) are of eleven types according to the number of the *pratimās* to which they might attain as laymen. But they are divided into three classes for the purposes of penance. The *jaghanya* (small, *i.e.*, inferior) class covers the first six *pratimās;* the middling (*madhyama*), those from the seventh to the ninth, and the *utkriṣta* (superior), the last two. The rule is that half the penance of the saint's is to be given to the superior layman ; half of that to the middling; and half of that half to the inferior householder.[1] According to another rule, half of the saint's penance should be fixed for the superior type of the layman, a third of his (the saint's) for the middling type, and a quarter, for the inferior class.[2] In the case of the superior laymen, who have deserved it, the *mūla* penance should be taken, as far as possible, from the same preceptor (saint) who had originally initiated them.[3]

Special or additional rules applicable to the inferior class of laymen are as follows :—

For killing a cow, a woman, a child, a virtuous layman and a saint[4]	*mahāmaha* (special worship of the God Arhant) in addition to the other penance.

[1] Ch. 137. [2] Ch. 138. [3] Ch. 112.

For killing a cow [1]	11 fasts preceded and followed by a *ṣaṣṭha*.

NOTE.—*The layman is also required to eat rice-water with rice grains* (*kānji*) on the intervening days, between the fasts, from his hand (not in a plate).[2] He should also live controlling his senses, and perform *pratikramaṇa* three times—morning, noon and evening—daily, followed by a *kāyotsarga* of 300 full "breaths," and should also perform one *kāyotsarga* at night.[3]

For killing a woman	twice the penance provided for the killing of a cow.
For killing a child	twice the penance for killing a woman.
For killing a man	twice of that for a child.
For killing a man devoted to one of the wrong faiths	twice that for killing a man.
For killing a *Brāhmaṇa*	twice that for killing a person devoted to a wrong faith.
For killing a Jaina layman	twice that for killing a *Brāhmaṇa*.
For killing a Jaina saint[4]	twice that for killing a Jaina layman.

NOTE.—On the termination of the penance the transgressor should bathe in the washing of a consecrated Jaina Statue, worship the God Arhant, and give away suitable gifts of four kinds to the deserving people.[5] He should shave off his hair and then enter his house.[6] The four kinds of gifts are the gifts of food, medicine, knowledge and 'protection.'

For killing two-sensed, three-sensed and four-sensed forms of life [7]	one fast.

[1] Ch. 140. [2] Ch. 141. [3] Ch. 142. [4] Ch. 143.
[5] Ch. 144. [6] Ch. 145. [7] Ch. 146.

For the violation of the second, third, fourth and fifth vows[1] ... ... one *ṣaṣṭha.*

For the transgressions of the *guṇa* and *sikshā* vows[1] ... ... one *upavāsa.*

For defiling faith or knowledge[1] ... ... the worship of the *Jina* (Arhant).

NOTE.—There are five different degrees of transgressions which should be kept in mind in awarding the penance :—

(1) *atikarma* which is the sinful intent;
(2) *vyatikarma* which signifies preparation for the act;
(3) *atichāra* which is the doing of something in the nature of a step towards its commission;
(4) *anāchāra* which is the 'regretful' violation of a vow;
(5) *abhoga* which means abandoning oneself to the vice.

The example of an old bull that would like to graze in a paddock is given in the Scripture to illustrate these differences. The intention to graze is *atikarma;* if the animal put his muzzle in a hole in the field's boundary to get to the grass it would be *vyatikarma;* if he jump over the wall, it would be *atichāra;* if he pull one mouthful and jump out again it would be *anāchāra;* but if he begins to graze at leisure and pleasure, that is fearlessly, it would be *abhoga.* These five kinds of transgressions apply to all the twelve vows of the layman.[1] In awarding penance notice might well be taken of these classes and sub-classes of sins.

1 Ch. 146.

For taking (eating or drinking) semen, urine, fæces, honey, flesh, wine, and improper (*abhakshya*) food [1]

(a) through indifference or ignorance ... one *ṣaṣṭha* ;
(b) deliberately (rather boastingly) ... twelve fasts.

For eating the five kinds of *udambaras*
(a) through indifference or negligence ... one fast.
(b) deliberately [1] ... ... twelve fasts

NOTE.—This is applicable to the case of an inferior layman.

For touching (needlessly) the corpse of a man who has been killed or who has died of an accident, or a body with a festering sore, full of worms [2] ... ... 6 fasts.

For co-habiting with one's daughter, mother, sister, or other nearly related females, or with a *pariah* or a base-born girl [3] ... 32 fasts.

For purchasing stolen property [4] ... ... one *kalyānaka*.

NOTE.—No penance is necessary if the things are purchased without guilty intent, *e.g.*, when more costly things are mixed up with less costly ones, without regard to price, and are purchased at one rate.

For taking more food than one can eat

(a) if enough to make a whole meal is left ... ... one *upavāsa* ;
(b) if a half or a third of a whole meal is left ... ... one *āchāmla* ;
(c) in all other cases [5] ... ... one *purumandala*.

NOTE.—The above rule is given in the text amongst the rules applicable to saints. It does not however apply to a saint, but might do so to the case of a nun. It can also apply to the case of a householder of the type of a *kshullaka*. The *kshullakas* are the superior type of laity who retain only one piece of cloth; they do not eat

1 Ch. 147. 2 Ch. 149. 3 Ch. 150.
4 S. 49. 5 S. 55.

standing; nor do they practise the *ātāpana*,[1] the *vṛiksha*[2] *mūla* and the *abhrāvakāsha*[3] *yoga* austerities.[4] The *kshullaka* belonging to the three higher *varṇas* (castes) who claim purity of descent on both the paternal and maternal sides, that is to say, both of whose parents are of the same *varṇa*, is entitled to be admitted into *sannyāsa* if he wishes to observe the *sallekhanā* vow; but not if he be descended from a mixed marriage, even though of the higher *varṇas*.[5] The instance of Prince Abhaya Kumar, however, shows this practice to be of recent origin as already noted. Only a *bhojya śudra* can be allowed to become a *kshullaka* and an *ellaka*, not the *abhojya* ("the uneatable with").[6] The *kshullaka* may get himself shaved or have his hair cut with scissors, or pluck them out with his own hands; he may eat from his own hand or from a plate. He wears only one piece of cloth.[7] The *ellaka* is the superior type of the *kshullaka* who retains only the loin-strip.

THE PERIOD OF UNCLEANNESS

The following periods have been fixed for 'uncleanness' consequent on death :—

For the death of a *sva-jana* (literally own man) ... ...

(a) if a *Brāhmaṇa* ... ... 5 days
(b) if a *Kshatriya* ... ... 10 days
(c) if a *Vaiśya*[8] ... ... 12 days

NOTE.—According to other *āchāryas*, a *Brāhmaṇa* becomes clean after ten days; and a *Kshatriya* after only five days. There is no uncleanness if the dead *sva-jana*, be a child, or a man belonging to a wrong faith who has performed *sannyasa marana* (*sallekhanā*). There is no need for observing the rule of uncleanness when a person dies of drowning or by fire."[9]

1 The *ātāpana* is a form of *yoga* austerity in which the *yogi* remains in the sun for a period fixed.

2 The *vṛiksha mūla* is another form of *yoga* austerity in which the *yogi* remains under a tree for a fixed period.

3 The *abhrāvakāśa* signifies a form of austerity in which the *yogi* spends all his time in but not under shade.

4 Ch. 155. 5 Ch. 113. 6 Ch. 154. 7 Ch. 156.
8 Ch. 153. 9 S. 154.

ॐ

श्रीवीतरागाय नमः

श्रीमद्-गुरुदासाचार्यविरचित-

प्रायश्चित्त-समुच्चयः

१—संज्ञाधिकारः

संयमामलसद्रत्नगम्भीरोदरसागरान् ।
श्रीगुरूनादराद्वन्दे रत्नत्रयविशुद्धये ॥१॥
भावा यत्राभिधीयन्ते हेयादेयविकल्पतः ।
अप्यतीचारसंशुद्धिस्तं श्रुताब्धिमभिष्टुवे ॥२॥
पारंपर्यक्रमायातं रत्नत्रयविशोधनम् ।
संक्षेपात् संप्रवक्ष्यामि प्रायश्चित्तसमुच्चयम् ॥३॥
प्रायश्चित्तं तपः प्राज्यं येन पापं पुरातनम् ।
क्षिप्रं संक्षीयते तस्मात्तत्र यत्नो विधीयताम् ॥४॥
प्रायश्चित्तेऽसति स्यान्न चारित्रं तद्विना पुनः ।
न तीर्थं न विना तीर्थान्निवृत्तिस्तद् वृथा व्रतम् ॥५॥
रहस्यं छेदनं दंडो मलापनयनं नयः ।
प्रायश्चित्ताभिधानानि व्यवहारो विशोधनम् ॥६॥
प्रायश्चित्तविधिं सूरिरजानानः कलंकयेत् ।
आत्मानमथ शिष्यं च दोषजातान्न शोधयेत् ॥७॥
स्वस्थाने मासिकं मूलगुणो मूलममी इति ।
पंचकल्याणपर्याया गुरुमासोऽथ पंचमः ॥८॥

नीरसेऽप्यथ वाचाम्ले क्षमणे वा विशोधिते।
ज्ञात्वा पुरुषसत्वादि लघुर्वा सान्तरो गुरुः ॥९॥
पंचस्वथापनीतेषु भिन्नमासः स एव वा।
उपवासैस्त्रिभिः षष्ठमपि कल्याणकं भवेत् ॥१०॥
कायोत्सर्गप्रमाणाय नमस्कारा नवोदिताः।
उपवासस्तनूत्सर्गैर्भवेद् द्वादशकैस्त्रकैः ॥११॥
आचाम्लेन सपादोनस्ततःपादः पुरुमंडलात्।
एकस्थानात्तदर्धं स्यादेवं निर्विकृतेरपि ॥१२॥
अष्टोत्तरशतं पूर्णं यो जपेदपराजितम्।
मनोवाक्कायगुप्तः सन् प्रोषधफलमश्नुते ॥१३॥
षोडशाक्षरविद्यायां स्यात्तदेव शतद्वये।
त्रिशत्यां षड्वर्णेषु चतसृष्वपि चतुःशते ॥१४॥
अकारं परमं वीजं जपेद्यः शतपंचकम्।
प्रोषधं प्राप्नुयात् सम्यक् शुद्धबुद्धिरतंद्रितः ॥१५॥

२—प्रतिसेवाधिकारः

प्रतिसेवा, ततः कालः क्षेत्राहारोपलब्धयः।
पुमांश्छेदो विपश्चिद्भिर्विधिः षोढात्र कीर्त्यते ॥१६॥
निमित्तादनिमित्ताच्च प्रतिसेवा द्विधा मता।
कारणात् षोडशोद्दिष्टा अष्टभंगास्तथेतरे ॥१७॥
सहेतुकः सकृत्कारी सानुवीची प्रयत्नवान्।
सद्विपक्षा द्विकाः सन्ति षोडशाऽन्योऽन्यताडिताः ॥१८॥
भंगायामप्रमाणेन लघुर्गुरुरिति क्रमात्।
प्रस्तारेऽत्राक्षनिक्षेपो द्विगुणो द्विगुणास्ततः ॥१९॥
विशुद्धः प्रथमोऽन्त्योऽपि सर्वथा शुद्धिवर्जितः।
भंगाश्चतुर्दशान्ये तु सर्वे भाज्या भवन्त्यमी ॥२०॥
आगाढकारणे कश्चित्क्लेषाशुद्धोऽपि शुद्ध्यति।
विशुद्धोऽपि पदैः शेषैरनागाढे न शुद्ध्यति ॥२१॥

अकारणो सकृत्कारी सानुवीचिः प्रयत्नवान् ।
तद्विपक्षा द्विका एतेऽप्यष्टावन्योन्यसंगुणाः ॥२२॥
अष्टाप्येते न संशुद्धा आद्यः शुद्धतरस्ततः ।
अविशुद्धतरास्त्वन्ये भंगाः सप्तापि सर्वदा ॥२३॥
प्रतिसेवाविकल्पानां त्रयोविंशतिमामृषन् ।
गुरुं लाघवमालोच्य छेदं दद्याद्यथायथम् ॥२४॥
द्रव्ये क्षेत्रेऽथ काले वा भावे विज्ञाय सेवनाम् ।
क्रमशः सम्यगालोच्य यथाप्राप्तं प्रयोजयेत् ॥२५॥
नीरसः पुरुमंडमाप्याचाम्लं चैकसंस्थितिः ।
क्षमणं च तपो देयमेकैकं द्व्यादिमिश्रकम् ॥२६॥
आलोचनादिकं योग्ये कायोत्सर्गोऽथ सर्वकम् ।
तपः आदि कचिद्देयं यथा वक्ष्ये विधिं तथा ॥२७॥
यदभीक्ष्णं निषेव्येत परिहर्तुं न याति यत् ।
यद्दोषश्च भवेत्तत्र कायोत्सर्गो विशोधनम् ॥२८॥
अपमृष्टपरामर्शे कंडूत्याकुञ्चनादिषु ।
जल्लखेलादिकोत्सर्गे कायोत्सर्गः प्रकीर्तितः ॥२९॥
तंतुच्छेदादिके स्तोके संक्लिष्टे हस्तकर्मणि ।
मनोमासिकसेवायां कायोत्सर्गः प्रकीर्तितः ॥३०॥
मृदाथवा स्थिरैर्बीजैर्हरिद्भिस्त्रसकायकैः ।
संघट्टने विपश्चिद्भिः कायोत्सर्गः प्रकीर्तितः ॥३१॥
पांशुचाक्षिप्तपदस्तोये विशेद् वा विपरीतकः ।
पुरुमंडलमाप्नोति कल्याणं कर्दमार्द्रपात् ॥३२॥
हरित्सु सकृच्छिन्ने छिन्ने चानन्तके त्रसे ।
पुरुमंडलमाचाम्लमेकस्थानमनुक्रमात् ॥३३॥
प्रत्येकेऽनन्तकाये वा त्रसे वाथ प्रमादतः ।
आचाम्लं चैकसंस्थानं क्षमणं च यथाक्रमम् ॥३४॥
व्यापन्ने सन्निधौ देया निष्प्रमादप्रमादिनोः ।
पंच स्युर्नीरसाहाराश्चैकं कल्याणकं त्रसे ॥३५॥

आभीक्ष्ण्ये पंचकल्याणं पंचाक्षे चापि दर्पतः ।
प्रमादेनैककल्याणं सकृदप्युपयोगतः ॥३६॥
संस्तरे यदि पंचाक्षो व्यापद्येताप्रमादतः ।
पंच निर्विकृतान्येककल्याणं सप्रमादतः ॥३७॥
आवासद्वारमूले चेत्पंचाक्षो विगतासुकः ।
तन्निष्क्रान्तप्रविष्टानामेककल्याणकं भवेत् ॥३८॥
विरतेभ्यो गृहस्थेभ्यो न यत्नकथिते हते ।
वृश्चिकादौ गृहस्थेन क्षमणं पंचकं क्रमात् ॥३९॥
विरतेभ्यो गृहस्थेभ्यो न यत्नाभिहिते हते ।
सर्पादौ तु गृहस्थे न कल्याणं मासिकं पृथक् ॥४०॥
संयतेभ्यः प्रयत्नेन विषीति कथिते हते ।
गृहस्थेनापि संशुद्धो वाक्समित्या युतो यतः ॥४१॥
आगाढकारणाद्वह्निर्निर्वाप्यानीयमानकः ।
पंच स्युर्नीरसाहाराः कल्याणं वा प्रमादिनि ॥४२॥
ग्लानार्थं तापयन् द्रव्यं वह्निज्वालां यदि स्पृशेत् ।
पंच स्यू रूक्षभक्तानि कल्याणं च मुहुर्मुहुः ॥४३॥
विभावसोः समारंभं वैद्यादेशाद्यदि स्वयम् ।
अनापृच्छ्यातुरं कुर्यात् पंचकल्याणमश्नुते ॥४४॥
विदध्याद् ग्लानमापृच्छ्य वैयावृत्यकरोऽथवा ।
तस्य स्यादेककल्याणं पंचकल्याणमातुरे ॥४५॥
कारणादामलादीनि सेवमानो न दुष्यति ।
बिल्वपेश्यादि चाश्नाति शुद्धः कल्याणभागथ ॥४६॥
रसधान्यपुलाकं वा पलांडुसूरणादिकम् ।
कल्याणमश्नुतेऽश्नन्वा मासं कर्कोलकादिकम् ॥४७॥
कान्दर्प्ये यन्मृषावादे मिथ्याकारेण शुद्धयति ।
अननुज्ञातसंशून्यखलादिकमलोज्झने ॥४८॥
जघन्यं तुल्यमूल्येन गृह्णानोऽपि विशुद्धयति ।
उत्कृष्टं मध्यमं वाथ गृह्णतो मासिकं भवेत् ॥४९॥

तृणपंचकसेवायां स्याद्विविंकृतिपंचकम् ।
कृष्याजिनासनानां च कल्याणं पंचकं सकृत् ॥५०॥
पंचकेऽप्रतिलेख्यस्य मासः स्यात् सेवने सकृत् ।
संदंशच्छेदसूच्यादिधारणे शुद्ध एव हि ॥५१॥
संस्तरस्य निषद्यायास्तदिकाया उपासने ।
घटीसंपुटपट्टस्य फलकस्य न दूषिका ॥५२॥
उपधौ विस्मृतेऽप्युच्चैर्मध्यमेऽथ जघन्यके ।
क्षमणं कंजिकाहारं पुरुमंडलमेव च ॥५३॥
दुःस्थापितोपधेर्नाशे सर्वत्रोत्कृष्टमध्यमे ।
जघन्ये मासिकं षष्ठं चतुर्थं कंजिकाशनम् ॥५४॥
पुरुषार्धं तदर्धं वा स्वल्पान्नं वा समुत्सृजन् ।
अभोजनमथाचाम्लं पुरुमंडलमश्नुते ॥५५॥
आगंतुकगृहे सुप्तः सार्द्रसोदकवह्निके ।
सागारैरप्यवेलायां शुद्ध एष स चेत्सकृत् ॥५६॥
वर्षास्वतुच्छकार्येण हिमे ग्रीष्मे लघीयसि ।
योजनानि दश द्वे च कार्ये गच्छन्न दोषभाक् ॥५७॥
ऋतुबंधमतिक्रामेन्मासेनाकारणाद्यदि ।
लघुमासो गुरुः स स्यात् सर्ववर्षाविभेदिनि ॥५८॥
दर्पतः पंचकल्याणं सारीनाल्यादिकेलिषु ।
हेतुवादे तु कल्याणं शुद्धो वा विजये सति ॥५९॥
धूलिप्रहेलिकागाथाचक्रकूलान्ताक्षरोक्तिषु ।
सूत्रपाशविपाशेऽपि पुरुमंडलमीरितम् ॥६०॥
धातुवादेऽथ योगादिदर्शने द्रव्यनाशने ।
स्वपक्षैर्वीक्षिते देयं कल्याणं मासिकं परैः ॥६१॥
समासाद्यंगसंघर्षसूत्रकंदुककेलिषु ।
पणनं मल्लपिच्छाहिजंघावीणादिवादने ॥६२॥
स्वपक्षैर्वीक्षिते देयाद्भूतक्रीडाप्रदर्शने ।
पुरुमंडलमुद्दिष्टं कल्याणं च परेक्षिते ॥६३॥ युग्मम्

मनसा काममापन्ने निंदातीव्राभिलाषिणि ।
मासो मैथुनमापन्ने चतुर्मासा गुरुकृता. ॥६४॥
मासः सौन्दर्यवीर्यार्थं रसायननिषेवणे ।
विशुद्धो द्विविधे हासे कल्याणं तु सकुत्कुचे ॥६५॥
वृक्षरिस्त्रसगर्ताम्बु परिहर्तुं विलंघने ।
मार्गे सत्यपि कल्याणं विशुद्धः पथि वर्जितः ॥६६॥
मोट्टायनांगुलिस्फोटे पुरुमर्दोऽपवीक्षणे ।
कल्याणं पंचकल्याणं कटाक्षेऽसंज्ञिवीक्षते ॥६७॥
ज्ञानगर्वादिभिर्मत्तो रत्निनो योऽपमन्यते ।
तद्दर्पदोषघाताय पंचकल्याणमश्नुते ॥६८॥
समुत्पन्नकषायोदूध्वस्ते मिथ्याकारः कषायके ।
स्यात्कल्याणमहोरात्रे मासिकं च ततः परम् ॥६९॥
विकथासु पुरुमर्दः स्यादाभीक्ष्ण्ये च पंचकम् ।
तात्पर्ये रुक्छ्रु तौ गर्हा कल्याणं निर्गते बहिः ॥७०॥
कृष्यभक्तं विजीवेऽपि सजीवे पुरुमंडलम् ।
आभीक्ष्ण्ये च निवृत्ते च ज्ञाते पंचकमुच्यते ॥७१॥
सेवमाने रसान् गृद्ध्या पंचकं वा न दोषता ।
शीतवातातपानेवं सेवमानो विशुद्ध्यति ॥७२॥
प्रावारसंस्तरासेवे संवाहे परिमर्दने ।
सर्वांगमर्दने चैवाहेतोः पंचकमंचति ॥७३॥
उच्छीर्षस्य विधानेऽपि प्रतिलेखस्य हृच्छदे ।
मस्तकावरणादेयं कल्याणं वा न दुष्यति ॥७४॥
छत्रोपानहसंसेवी शरीरावारकारकः ।
मार्गधर्मार्द्धि कल्याणं लभते शुद्ध एव वा ॥७५॥
शयानः प्रथमे यामे काले शुद्धेऽपि पंचकात् ।
शुद्धेऽथवा विसंशुद्धौ लभते पुरुमंडलम् ॥७६॥
शयालुर्दिवसे शेते चेत्कल्याणं समश्नुते ।
अतोऽन्यस्य भवेद्योग्यो भिन्नमासो विशुद्धये ॥७७॥

हस्तकर्मणि मासार्हं गुरौ लघुनि पंचकम् ।
शुद्धश्च पंचकं मासश्चतुर्मास्यां लघौ गुरौ ॥७८॥
पार्श्वस्थानुचरे बाह्यभृतिशिक्षणाकारणात् ।
करणीकाव्यशिक्षायै मिथ्याकारेऽथ पंचकम् ॥७९॥
व्याधौ सुदुस्सहे यत्नाद् भेषजे प्रासुके कृते ।
मिथ्याकारोऽथ कल्याणमयत्नान्मासपंचके ॥८०॥
समित्यासादने शोके मिथ्याकारश्चिरं धृते ।
अश्रुपाते च कल्याणं रसगृद्धे द्विलापिनि ॥८१॥
सचित्ताशंकिते भग्ने स्यादेकस्थितिदण्डनम् ।
बहुजीवे भवेन्निन्दा सजीवे भक्तवर्जनम् ॥८२॥
शय्यायामुपधौ पिंडे शंकायामुद्गमैर्हते ।
उत्पादैश्चतुर्मास्यां मासो मासेऽपि पंचकम् ॥८३॥
कल्याणमेषणादोषे दायके पुरुमण्डलम् ।
मिश्रेऽपरिणते मासो भिन्नः समनुवर्णितः ॥८४॥
निर्दोषोऽत्यंततात्पर्यादल्पानल्पे प्रलेपने ।
स्तोकेऽयत्नात्पुरुमर्दः कल्याणं बहुलेपने ॥८५॥
अल्पलेपे च यत्नेन पश्चात्कर्मणि शुद्धयति ।
अल्पलेपेऽप्ययत्नेन दंडनं पुरुमण्डलम् ॥८६॥
बहुलेपेऽप्ययत्नेन पंचकं वा न दोषयुक् ।
अयत्नेनोभयं (मे) वापि स्वस्थानेन विशुद्धयति ॥८७॥
ददत्याः संप्रमर्दाद्वे प्रत्येकानन्तकौ त्रसम् ।
पुरुमण्डलमाचाम्लमेकस्थानं निषेवते ॥८८॥
भीत्वोन्मार्गं प्रपद्येत तरुमारोहति क्षिपेत् ।
काष्ठादिकं बिलद्वारपिधाने पंचकं न वा ॥८९॥
पुरुमर्दो यतोऽयत्नाद्विडालादिप्रवेशने ।
क्षमणं लघुमासोऽथ स्तेनस्य वृषसूदने ॥९०॥
मायंमाणान् विलोक्याश्वैश्चौरादीनेति पंचकम् ।
भिन्नमासमथो निन्दां पंचकं क्रियमाणकान् ॥९१॥

शब्दाद्भयानकाद्रूपादुत्त्रस्यैदंगमाक्षिपेत् ।
मिथ्याकारः स्वनिंदा वा पंचकं वा पलायने ॥९२॥
करांद्याकुंचने स्पर्शाद्व्यायामे पुरुमंडलम् ।
तत्क्षेपे पंचकं मासः पाषाणाद्य लघोर्गुरोः ॥९३॥
प्रधावयति धावेद्वा वर्षाद्वृक्षैरभित्रसन् ।
स्वनिंदा वाथ कल्याणं मासो लाघवदर्शिनि ॥९४॥
पिपीलिकादिभीमांसाधारणे स्यात्प्रतिक्रमः ।
चिरं क्रीडयतो देयं कल्याणं मलशोधनम् ॥९५॥
विद्यामीमांसने योगप्रयोगे प्रासुकैः कृते ।
शुद्ध्ये द्वयसंयुक्तैर्लघुमासं समश्नुते ॥९६॥
युंजानः संयते शुद्धो दिदृक्षुर्वीर्यमौषधेः ।
गृहस्थे मासमाप्नोति त्वार्यायां पंचकं न वा ॥९७॥
जिज्ञासुर्भेषजं वीर्यं सर्पादीनां प्रदर्शयेत् ।
मिथ्याकारो विपन्ने स्युश्चतुर्मासा गुरुकृताः ॥९८॥
साभोगे पादसंशुद्धा उद्धर्तादावभोजनम् ।
पंचकं च यथासंख्यं शृङ्गारे मासिकं विदुः ॥९९॥
सर्वभूरिषु भांडेषु मध्यमेष्वमध्यमेषु च ।
षष्ठं चतुर्थमेवैकस्थितिः सौवीरभोजनम् ॥१००॥
शुद्धेष्वपि च संशुद्धौ कात्स्न्येनाथ पृथक् पृथक् ।
शोभायै मासिकं चैवमापन्नेष्वप्यशुद्धेषु ॥१०१॥
अन्नपानविलिप्तं वा यावत्तावद्विशोधयन् ।
विशुद्धः कृत्स्नसंशुद्धौ मासिकं समुदाहृतम् ॥१०२॥
वृषादिवारणे शुद्धः स्याद्वर्षासु तु पंचकम् ।
सागारवसतौ स्तेनप्रवेशे जोषमास्थितः ॥१०३॥
वीक्ष्यमाणहृतौ मासः कल्याणमहृताहृतोः ।
वसतावनले स्तेनप्रविष्टे शब्दकृच्छुचिः ॥१०४॥
पश्चात्कर्मभयात् सम्यग्भग्नमुत्पतितं स्वयम् ।
संस्कुर्वन् प्रासुकैः शुद्धो वर्षाभ्यः पंचकं व्रजेत् ॥१०५॥

सम्यग्दृष्टिरिति स्नेहं वात्सल्याद्वितन्वञ्छुचिः ।
शय्यागारादिकस्यापि वैयावृत्त्ये विजन्तुकैः ॥१०६॥
अन्यतीर्थिगृहस्थेषु श्रावकज्ञातिकादिषु ।
वैयावृत्त्ये कृते शुद्धो यदि संयमसन्मुखः ॥१०७॥
अभ्युत्थास्यत्ययं हीति ज्ञात्वा पार्श्वस्थकादिकैः ।
समाचरन् शुचिः स्तोकं सर्वसंभोगभागपि ॥१०८॥
शुद्धोऽभिवंदमानोऽपि पार्श्वस्थगणिनं गणी ।
शेषानपि च शेषाश्च संघे अपथ मासिकम् ॥१०९॥
स्नेहमुत्पादयन् कुर्यात् सुवाग्भिर्धर्मभाषणम् ।
राजरक्षिकतत्प्राये संशुद्धो गणरक्षणात् ॥११०॥
अभ्युत्थानेऽभिगत्यादौ सागारेष्वन्यलिंगिषु ।
दीक्षादिकारणाच्छुद्धो गौरवान्मासमृच्छति ॥१११॥
अभ्युत्थानेऽथ वैद्यस्य ग्लानकारणसंश्रयात् ।
राजासन्नासनारोहे सूरिसूर्यो न दुष्यति ॥११२॥
भूपालेश्वरमुख्याद्याः पूजयन्त्यभिगम्य चेत् ।
शुद्धभावो विशुद्धः स्यात् गौरवे मासिकं भवेत् ॥११३॥
रससातमदे वृष्यरसस्पर्शार्थसेवने ।
च्युतेऽनात्मवशस्यापि पञ्चकल्याणमुच्यते ॥११४॥
उपसर्गे सगंधादेर्वेकताबूललेपनं
प्रत्याख्यानस्य भुक्तौ च गुरुमासोऽथ पंचकम् ॥११५॥
मैथुन रात्रिभुक्तौ च स्वस्थानं परिकीर्तितम् ।
स्त्रियोः संधौ प्रसुप्तस्य मनोरोधाच्च दूषणम् ॥११६॥
आवश्यकाकुर्वाणः स्वाध्यायान् लघुमासिकम् ।
एकैकं वाप्रलेखायां कल्याणं दंडमश्नुते ॥११७॥
वन्दनायास्तनूत्सर्गेऽप्येकादौ विस्मृते त्रिषु ।
पुरुमंडलमाचाम्लं क्षमणं च यथाक्रमम् ॥११८॥
एकादिके गुरोरादौ कायोत्सर्गस्य पारणे ।
पुरुमण्डलमाचाम्लं क्षमणं च यथाक्रमम् ॥११९॥

कारणाद्वा गुरोः पश्चात् कायोत्सर्गं समापयेत् ।
सकृद्द्वित्रिः पुरुमर्त्योऽप्याचाम्लं चैकसंस्थितिः ॥१२०॥
आसेधिकां निषद्यां वा न कुर्यात्स्थ्यादिके निशि ।
अनाहारोऽम्लभुक्तिश्च पुरुमंडलमेव च ॥१२१॥
आसेधिकां निषद्यां च मिथ्याकारं निमंत्रणम् ।
इच्छाकारं न यः कुर्यात्तद्दंडः पुरुमंडलम् ॥१२२॥
उत्कृष्टं मध्यमं नीचमदत्तं स्वीकरोति यः ।
उपधिं लघुमासोऽस्य पंचकं पुरुमंडलम् ॥१२३॥
संज्ञाविहारभिक्षासु पुरुमंडलमीडितम् ।
क्रोशादिग्रामगतावप्यनापृच्छ्य गुरुं गते ॥१२४॥
साधारणाशनासेवे स्थापनावेश्मवेशने ।
ज्ञात्वा संज्ञिकुलादीनि पूर्ववेशिनि पंचकम् ॥१२५॥
अन्यदत्तोपधेः स्थानमन्यो गत्वा तमाददत् ।
मासिकं लभते मूलं रूपव्यत्ययकारिणः ॥१२६॥
अतिबालमलंवृद्धं दीक्षयन् मासमश्नुते ।
वसतिं च व्यवच्छिन्दन् छेदे मूले गणी तपः ॥१२७॥
एवं भावोपयुक्तेषु मासिकं समुदाहृतम् ।
छेदे मूले च संप्राप्ते तप एव गणेशिनः ॥१२८॥
एवमादि तपो देयं शेषं चापि यथोचितम् ।
प्रतिसेवासु सर्वासु सम्यगालोच्य सूरिणा ॥१२९॥

३—कालाधिकारः

शीतः साधारणो धर्मस्त्रेधा कालः प्रकीर्तितः ।
उत्कृष्टं मध्यमं नीचं तत्र भाज्यं तपो भवेत् ॥१३०॥
वर्षासु द्वादशं देयं दशमं च हिमागमे ।
अष्टमं ग्रीष्मकाले स्यादेतदुत्कर्षतस्तपः ॥१३१॥

वर्षासु दशमं देयं अष्टमं च हिमागमे ।
षष्ठं स्याद् ग्रीष्मकालेऽपि तप एतद्धि मध्यमम् ॥१३२॥
वर्षाकालेऽष्टमं देयं षष्ठमेव हिमागमे ।
चतुर्थं ग्रीष्मकाले स्यात्तप एव जघन्यकम् ॥१३३॥
अथवा द्विविधः कालो गुरुर्लघुरिति क्रमात् ।
शरद्वसन्ततापाः स्युर्गुरवो लघवः परे ॥१३४॥
लघुर्द्वंद्वो गुरुर्द्वंद्वो गुरुकालस्तपो गुरुः ।
गुरुरन्यतरः पंच भंगाः कालतपोद्वयात् ॥१३५॥

४—क्षेत्राधिकारः

क्षेत्रं नानाविधं ज्ञेयं गणेऽक्लेशाटता भुवम् ।
अथवा दशधा क्षेत्रं विज्ञेयं हि समासतः ॥१३६॥
अनूपं जांगलं क्षेत्रं भक्तकल्माषशक्तुयुक् ।
रसधान्यपुलाकं च यवागूकंदमूलदम् ॥१३७॥
शीतलं यद्भवेद्यत्र रससंसृष्टभोजनम् ।
तत्रोत्कृष्टं तपो देयमुष्णे रूक्षे तु हीनकम् ॥१३८॥

५—आहारलाभाधिकारः

यत्रोत्कृष्टो भवेल्लाभः तत्रोत्कृष्टं तपो भवेत् ।
मध्यमेऽपीषदूनं च रूक्षे क्षमणवर्जितम् ॥१३९॥

६—पुरुषाधिकारः

धृति सेवां च कालं च क्षेत्रमौषधिलंभनम् ।
अनुसृज्य तपो देयं पुमांसं च गणेशिना ॥१४०॥
अभ्राढ्योऽथ मृदुगंर्वी गीतार्थश्चेतरोऽल्पवित् ।
दुर्बलो नीचसंघातः सर्वपूर्वस्तथार्यिका ॥१४१॥

गर्वितो द्विविधो ज्ञेयो दीक्षया तपसा बली ।
छेदेन छेद्यमानोऽपि पर्यायी गर्वितो भवेत् ॥१४२॥
तपोबली तपोदाने समर्थोऽहमिति स्मयी ।
तस्मात्तद्दोषमोषार्थं विपरीतं तपो भवेत् ॥१४३॥
मृदुश्छेदे च मूले च दीयमाने प्रहृष्यति ।
वंद्यो हि सर्वथा साधुस्तत्तस्मै दीयते तपः ॥१४४॥
प्राज्यं तपो न कुर्वाणः किं शुद्ध्येच्छेदमूलतः ।
गुर्वाज्ञामात्रतोऽश्रद्दधाने देयं तपस्ततः ॥१४५॥
गीतार्थे स्यात्तपः सर्वं स्थापनारहितोऽपरः ।
छेदो मूलं परीहारे मासश्चाल्पश्रुतेऽपि च ॥१४६॥
देहबल्यबलो धृत्या धृतिबल्यंगदुर्बलः ।
द्वाभ्यामपि बली कश्चित् कश्चिद् द्वितयदुर्बलः ॥१४७॥
सर्वं तपो बलोपेते धृत्या हीने धृतिप्रदम् ।
देहदुर्बलमाश्रित्य लघु देयं द्विवर्जिते ॥१४८॥
अन्त्यसंहननोपेतो बलवानागमान्तगः ।
तस्य देयं तपः सर्वं परिहारेऽपि मूलगः ॥१४९॥
आदिसंहननः सर्वगुणो योऽजितनिद्रकः ।
देयं सर्वं तपस्तस्य पारंचेऽप्यनुपस्थितिः ॥१५०॥
नवपूर्वधरो श्राद्धो वैराग्यधृतिमानजित् ।
परिणामसमग्रोऽपि योऽनुपस्थानभागसौ ॥१५१॥
आप्रश्नालोचने तस्य सदैव गुरुसन्निधौ ।
वंदनादिप्रकुर्वाणः प्रतिवंदनवर्जितः ॥१५२॥
गुणैरेतैः समग्रोऽसौ जघन्योत्कृष्टमध्यमाम् ।
पौराणिकीं गुणश्रेणिं निःशेषामभिपूरयेत् ॥१५३॥
श्रद्धाद्या ये गुणाः पूर्वमनुपस्थानवर्णिताः ।
पारंचिकेऽपि ते किन्तु कृतकृत्योऽधिसंहतिः ॥१५४॥
सर्वगुणसमग्रस्य देयं पारंचिकं भवेत् ।
व्युत्सृष्टस्यापि येनास्याशुद्धभावो न जायते ॥१५५॥

पंचदोषोपसृष्टस्य पारंचिकमनूदितम् ।
व्युत्सृष्टो विहरेद्देष सधर्मरहितस्थितौ ॥१५६॥
आदिसंहननो धीरो दशपूर्वकृतश्रमः ।
जितनिद्रो गुणाधारस्तस्य पारंचिकं विदुः ॥१५७॥
आर्यायाः स्यात्तपः सर्वं स्थापनापरिवर्जितम् ।
सप्तमासमपि प्राज्यं न पिंछच्छेदमूलगम् ॥१५८॥
प्रियधर्मा बहुज्ञानः कारणावृत्यसेवकः ।
ऋजुभावो विपक्षैस्तैर्द्विकैर्द्वात्रिंशदाहताः ॥१५९॥
द्वात्रिंशत्प्रियधर्माद्या अष्टाचार्यादिकाः पुनः ।
गर्विताद्या दशोद्दिष्टास्तेभ्यो देयं यथोचितम् ॥१६०॥
तेऽथवा पंचधोद्दिष्टा स्थानेष्वेतेष्वनुक्रमात् ।
आत्मोभयतरावन्यतरशक्तश्च नोभयः ॥१६१॥
परतरोऽपि निर्दिष्टस्त एवं पंच पूरुषाः ।
यथान्यायं तथैतेऽपि सप्त भाज्या गणेशिना ॥१६२॥
प्रायश्चित्तं गुरूद्दिष्टमग्लानः सन् करोति यः ।
वैयावृत्त्यं न रोचेत स आत्मतर ईरितः ॥१६३॥
प्रायश्चित्तं गुरूद्दिष्टं सुबह्वपि करोति यः ।
वैयावृत्त्यं च शुद्धात्मा ह्युभयतरोऽसौ प्रकीर्तितः ॥१६४॥
सर्वांगजातरोमांचो वैयावृत्त्यं तपो महत् ।
लाभद्वयं सुमन्वानः श्रेष्ठित्वे पुत्रलाभवत् ॥१६५॥
वैयावृत्त्यं समाधत्स्व तपो वेति गणीरितः ।
तत एकतरं धत्ते स्वेच्छयान्यतरः स्मृतः ॥१६६॥
वैयावृत्त्यं न यो वोढुं प्रायश्चित्तमपि क्षमः ।
दुर्बलो धृतिदेहाभ्यामलब्धिर्नोभयः स तु ॥१६७॥
दीयमानं तपः श्रुत्वा भयादुद्विजते मुहुः ।
प्रोद्वृत्तपाण्डुरश्च सन् म्लानिमेति प्रकंपते ॥१६८॥
वैमनस्यं समाधत्ते रोगमाप्नोति दुर्बलः ।
प्राणत्यागं विधत्ते वा श्रामण्याद्वा पलायते ॥१६९॥

प्रायश्चित्तं न शक्नोति कुर्याच्च व्यावृतिं बहु ।
दुर्बलस्तनुधैर्याभ्यां लब्धिमान् परशक्तिकः ॥१७०॥
द्विप्रकाराः पुमांसोऽथ सापेक्षा निरपेक्षकाः ।
निर्व्यपेक्षाः समर्थाः स्युराचार्याद्यास्तथेतरे ॥१७१॥
गीतार्थाः कृतकृत्याश्च निर्व्यपेक्षा भवन्त्यमी ।
आलोचनादिका, तेषामष्टधा शुद्धिरिष्यते ॥१७२॥
तेऽप्रमत्ताः सदा सन्तो दोषं जातं कथंचन ।
तत्क्षणादपकुर्वन्ति नियमेनात्मसाक्षिकम् ॥१७३॥
धैर्यसंहननोपेताः स्वातंत्र्याद्योगधारिणः ।
तद्वह्वपि समुत्पन्नं वहन्ति निरनुग्रहम् ॥१७४॥
आलोचनोपयुक्ता यच्छुध्यन्त्यालोचनात्ततः ।
कृत्वाशेषं च मूलान्तं शुध्यन्ति स्वयमेव ते ॥१७५॥
आचार्यो वृषभो भिक्षुरिति सापेक्षास्त्रिधा ।
गीतार्थौ वृषभः सूरिः कृत्यकृत्येतरौ पुनः ॥१७६॥
गीतार्थश्चेतरो भिक्षुः कृतकृत्येतरस्तयोः ।
आद्यः स्यादपरो द्वेधाधिगतश्चेतरोऽपि च ॥१७७॥
द्विधानधिगताभिख्यः स्यात्स्थिरास्थिरभेदतः ।
अत्राद्यास्वनधिगते वांछैवाऽस्थिरनामनि ॥१७८॥
कल्प्याकल्प्यं न जानाति नानिषेवितसेवितम् ।
अल्पानल्पं न बुध्येत तेनेच्छाऽबोधनेऽस्थिरे ॥१७९॥
कर्मोदयवशाद्दोषोऽधिगतेषु भवेद्यदि ।
तेषां स्याद्दशधा शुद्धिरागमाभ्यनुरागतः ॥१८०॥

७—छेदाधिकारः

प्रायश्चित्तं तपः श्लाघ्यं येन पापं विशुद्ध्यति ।
प्रायश्चित्तं समाप्नोति तेनोक्तं दशधेह तत् ॥१८१॥

प्रायश्चित्तविधावत्र यथाविभ्यन्त्रमाश्रितः ।
ज्ञातव्यं शुद्धियुक्तेन तदेतद्व्याघोष्यते ॥१८२॥
आलोचना प्रतिक्रान्तिर्द्वयं त्यागो विसर्जनम् ।
तपः छेदोऽपि मूलं च परिहारोऽभिरोचनम् ॥१८३॥
करणीयेषु योगेषु छद्मस्थत्वेन सन्मुनेः ।
उपयुक्तस्य दोषेषु शुद्धिरालोचना भवेत् ॥१८४॥
संज्ञोद्भ्रान्तविहारादावीर्यासमितिसंयतः ।
यो गुप्तिष्वप्रमत्तश्च निर्दोषोऽपि च संयमे ॥१८५॥
आलोचनापरीणामो यावदायाति नो गुरुम् ।
तावदेव स नो शुद्धः समालोच्य विशुध्यति ॥१८६॥
ये विहर्तुं विनिष्क्रान्ता गणाच्चरणसंयताः ।
आगतानां पुनस्तेषां शुद्धिरालोचना भवेत् ॥१८७॥
अन्यसंघगतानां च विशुद्धाचारधारिणाम् ।
उपसंपत्समेतानां शुद्धिरालोचना भवेत् ॥१८८॥
मनसाऽवद्यमापन्नो वाचाऽऽसाद्य गुरूनथ ।
उपयुक्तो वधे चापि प्राग्भवेत्तन्निवर्तनम् ॥१८९॥
तत्क्षणोद्वेगयुक्तस्य पश्चात्तापमुपेयुषः ।
स्वयमेवात्मसाक्षि स्यात्प्रायश्चित्तं विशोधनम् ॥१९०॥
वैयावृत्यक्रियाभ्रंशे छेदधोवातजृंभणे ।
दुःस्वप्ने विस्मृते वापि प्रायश्चित्तं प्रतिक्रमः ॥१९१॥
आभोगे वाप्यनाभोगे भिक्षाचर्यादिके क्वचित् ।
कथंचिदुत्थिते दंडे प्रायश्चित्तं प्रतिक्रमः ॥१९२॥
सूक्ष्मे दोषे न विज्ञाते छद्मस्थत्वेन चागसाम् ।
अनाभोगकृतानां च विशुद्धिस्तद्द्वयं भवेत् ॥१९३॥
दिवसे निशि पक्षेऽब्दे चतुर्मासोत्तमार्थके ।
शेषयानाभोगकार्येषु पदं यो युक्तयोगिनः ॥१९४॥
आलोचनोपयुक्तोऽपि निप्रमादो न वेत्त्यघम् ।
अनिगूहितभावश्च विशुद्धिस्तस्य तद्द्वयम् ॥१९५॥

शय्यामथोपधिं पिंडमादायैषणादूषणम् ।
प्रागविज्ञाय विज्ञाते प्रायश्चित्तं विवेचनम् ॥१९६॥
भक्तपानं विशुद्धं च समादायैषणाहतम् ।
तन्मात्रं वाथ सर्वं वा विशुद्धः संपरित्यजन् ॥१९७॥
भक्तपानं विशुद्धं च कोटिजुष्टमशुद्धियुक् ।
तन्मात्रं वाथ सर्वं वा विशुद्धः संपरित्यजन् ॥१९८॥
भक्तपानं विशुद्धं च भावदुष्टमशुद्धिमत् ।
सर्वमेवाथ तज्जुष्टं विशुद्धः संपरित्यजन् ॥१९९॥
भक्तपाने विशुद्धेऽपि क्षेत्रकालसमाश्रयात् ।
द्रव्यतः स्वीकृते रात्रौ विशुद्धस्तत्परित्यजन् ॥२००॥
प्रत्याख्यातं निषिद्धं यद्भक्तपानादिकं भवेत् ।
तत्पाणिपात्रास्यसंस्थं विशुद्धः परिवर्जयेत् ॥२०१॥
उत्पथेन प्रयातस्य सर्वत्राभावतः पथः ।
स्निग्धेन च विशीयाद्धविवद्यस्वप्नदर्शने ॥२०२॥
अस्तरस्य बहिर्देशेऽचक्षुषो विषये मृते ।
रात्रौ प्रमृष्टशय्यायां यत्नसुप्तोपवेशन ॥२०३॥
व्यापन्ने च त्रसे दृष्टे नद्याश्चागाढकारणात् ।
नावा निर्दोषयोत्तारे कायोत्सर्गो विशोधनम् ॥२०४॥
कन्यादौ निर्गते देहाद्देहासक्तमृते त्रसे ।
मक्षिकायां महावाते त्रसोत्थाने गतावपि ॥२०५॥
ओघानध्यासने रात्रावदृष्टे मलवर्जने ।
जीर्णोपधिपरित्यागे कायोत्सर्गो विशोधनम् ॥२०६॥
श्रुतस्कंधपरीवर्तस्वाध्यायस्य विसर्जने ।
कालाद्युल्लंघनं स्याच्चेत्कायोत्सर्गो विशोधनम् ॥२०७॥
दिवसे निशि पक्षेऽब्दे चतुर्मासोत्तमार्थके ।
मासे च द्रागनाभोगे कायोत्सर्गो विशोधनम् ॥२०८॥
एवमादितनूत्सर्गविधिमुल्लंघते यदा ।
अप्रासरछेदभूमिं च तपोभूमिं तदा श्रयेत् ॥२०९॥

नीरसः पुरुमंडश्चाप्याचाम्लं चैकसंस्थितिः ।
समर्थां च तपोदेयमेकैकं क्षुत्यादिभिश्चकम् ॥२१०॥
आषण्मासमिदं सर्वं सान्तरं च निरन्तरम् ।
अन्त्यतीर्थे न विधेत तत ऊर्ध्वं तपोऽधिकम् ॥२११॥
अपमृष्टे परामर्शे कंडूत्याकुंचनादिषु ।
अक्षलेखादिकोत्सर्गे पंचकं परिकीर्तितम् ॥२१२॥
दंडस्य च करोद्वृत्ते जंघासंपुटवेशने ।
कंटकाद्यननुज्ञातभंगादाने च पंचकम् ॥२१३॥
तंतुच्छेदादिके स्तोके दन्ताङ्गुल्यादिभिस्तथा ।
कृत्यादिकं दिवाऽध्यायो गुरुः स्यादग्निसेवने ॥२१४॥
प्रायश्चित्तं चरन् ग्लानो रोगाद्यातंकतो भवेत् ।
नीरोगस्य पुनस्तस्य दातव्यं पंचकं भवेत् ॥२१५॥
प्रायश्चित्तं वहन् सूरेः कार्यं संसाधयेत् सुधीः ।
परदेशे स्वदेशे वा दातव्यं तस्य पंचकम् ॥२१६॥
सालंबो यत्नतोऽध्वाने योऽभिव्रजति संयतः ।
निस्तीर्णस्य सतस्तस्य दातव्यं पंचकं भवेत् ॥२१७॥
नखच्छेदादिशस्त्रादि वास्याद्यैर्दंडकादिके ।
लघुगुर्वेकचत्वारः परश्वाद्यैश्च कर्तने ॥२१८॥
एकहस्तोपलाभ्यां च दोर्भ्यां मौद्गरमौसलात् ।
लघुगुर्वेकचत्वारः प्रभेदादिष्टकादितः ॥२१९॥
लघुं गुरुं तनुत्सर्गांस्त्रीनूर्ध्वमासतोऽश्नुते ।
आवश्यकमकुर्वाणश्चतुर्मासांस्तथाविधान् ॥२२०॥
आधाकर्मणि राजान्नस्यार्याभ्युत्थानतस्तथा ।
असंयतभिवादे च मासस्याधश्चतुर्गुरुः ॥२२१॥
नपुंसकस्य कुत्स्यस्य क्लीबाद्यस्य च दीक्षणे ।
वर्षापरस्य दीक्षायां षण्मासा गुरवः स्मृताः ॥२२२॥
तपोभूमिमतिक्रान्तो न प्राप्तो मूलभूमिकाम् ।
छेदार्हो तपसो भूमिं संप्रपद्येत भावतः ॥२२३॥

योऽतिचारो न शोध्येत तपसा भूरिणापि च।
पर्यायश्छिद्यते तेन छिन्नतावृक्षपत्रवत् ॥२२४॥
प्रव्रज्याकालतः कालच्छेदेन न्यूनतावहः।
मानापहारकश्छेद एकरात्रादिकः स तु ॥२२५॥
साधुसंघं समुत्सृज्य यो भ्रमत्येक एव हि।
तावत्कालोऽस्य पर्यायश्छिद्यते समुपेयुषः ॥२२६॥
सन् यथोक्तविधिः पूर्वमवसन्नः कुशीलवान्।
पार्श्वस्थो वाथ संसक्तो भूत्वा यो विहरत्यभीः ॥२२७॥
यावत्कालं भ्रमत्येष मुक्तमार्गो निरुत्सुकः।
तावत्कालोऽस्य पर्यायश्छिद्यते समुपेयुषः ॥२२८॥
पार्श्वस्थैर्विहरन् सार्धं सकृद्दोषनिषेवकः।
आषण्मासं तपस्तस्य भवेच्छेदस्ततः परम् ॥२२९॥
कृताधिकरणो गच्छेद्‌ऽनुपशान्तः प्रयाति यः।
तस्यच्छेदो भवेदेष स्वगणेऽन्यगणेऽपि च ॥२३०॥
प्रत्यहं छेदनं भिक्षोः पंचाहानि स्वके गणे।
वृषभस्य दशाहानि गणिनो दशपंच च ॥२३१॥
प्रत्यहं छेदनं भिक्षोर्दशाहानि परे गणे।
दशपंच वृषस्यापि विंशतिर्गणिनः पुनः ॥२३२॥
इत्यादिप्रतिसेवासुच्छेदः स्यादेवमादिकः।
छेदेनापि च संछिंद्याद्यावन्मूलं निरन्तरम् ॥२३३॥
छेदभूमिमतिक्रान्तः परिहारमनापिवान्।
प्रायश्चित्तं तदा मूलं संप्रपद्येत भावतः ॥२३४॥
श्रामण्यैकगुणा यस्माद्दोषान्नश्यन्ति कात्स्न्र्यतः।
भ्रष्टव्रतस्य तत्तस्य मूलं स्याद् व्रतरोपणम् ॥२३५॥
इत्वारिप्रव्रतभ्रष्टे त्यक्तावश्यककर्मणि।
अन्तर्वर्त्नीमुकुंसोपदीक्षणे मूलमुच्यते ॥२३६॥
तत्सूत्रं वर्णयेत् कामं जिनेन्द्रोक्तमिति ध्रुवम्।
यथाच्छंदो भवत्येष तस्य मूलं विलीयते ॥२३७॥

पार्श्वस्थादिचतुर्णां च तेषु प्रव्रजिताश्च ये ।
तेषां मूलं प्रदातव्यं यद्व्रतादि न तिष्ठति ॥२३८॥
अन्यतीर्थगृहस्थानां कांदर्प्यांछिंगकारिणः ।
मूलमेव प्रदातव्यमप्रमाणापराधिनः ॥२३९॥
इत्यादिप्रतिसेवासु मूलनिर्यातिनीष्वपि ।
हरिवंश्यादिदीक्षायां मूलं मूलाधिरोहणात् ॥२४०॥
मूलभूमिमतिक्रान्तः संप्राप्तः परिहारकम् ।
परिहारविधिं प्राज्ञः संप्रपद्येत भावतः ॥२४१॥
परिहार्यः स संघस्य स वा संघं परित्यजन् ।
परिहारो द्विधा सोऽपि पारंच्यप्यनुपस्थितिः ॥२४२॥
शिष्यकैरपि नो यस्य शुश्रूषावंदनादिकम् ।
अभ्युत्थानं विधीयेत कुर्वतः सोऽनुपस्थितिः ॥२४३॥
अन्यतीर्थ्यं गृहस्थं स्त्रीं सचित्तं वा सकर्मणः ।
चोरयन् बालकं भिक्षुं ताडयन्ननुपस्थितिः ॥२४४॥
द्वादशेन जघन्येन षण्मास्या च प्रकर्षतः ।
चरेद् द्वादशवर्षाणि गण एवानुपस्थितिः ॥२४५॥
एवमाद्यनुपस्थानप्रतिसेवाविलंघितः ।
प्रायश्चित्तं तु पारंचं प्रतिपद्येत भावतः ॥२४६॥
अपूज्यश्चाप्यसंभोगो दोषानुद्घुष्य गच्छतः ।
बहिष्कृतोऽपि तद्देशात् पारंचो तेन स स्मृतः ॥२४७॥
आसादनं वितन्वानस्तीर्थकृत्प्रभृतेरिह ।
सेवमानोऽपि दुष्टादीन् पारंचिकमुपाश्नुते ॥२४८॥
आचार्यांश्च महर्द्धींश्च तीर्थकृद्गणनायकान् ।
श्रुतं जैनं मतं भूयः पारं च्यासादयन् भवेत् ॥२४९॥
द्वादशेन जघन्येन षण्मास्या च प्रकर्षतः ।
चरेद् द्वादशवर्षाणि पारंची गणवर्जितः ॥२५०॥
राजापकारको राज्ञामुपकारकदीक्षकः ।
राजाग्रमहिषी सेवी पारंची संप्रकीर्तितः ॥२५१॥

अनाभोगेन मिथ्यात्वं संक्रान्तः पुनरागतः ।
तदेवच्छेदनं तस्य यस्सम्यगभिरोचते ॥२५२॥
यः साभोगेन मिथ्यात्वं संक्रान्तः पुनरागतः ।
जिनाचार्याज्ञया तस्य मूलमेव विधीयते ॥२५३॥
प्रायश्चित्तं जिनेन्द्रोक्तं रत्नत्रयविशोधनम् ।
प्रोक्तं संक्षेपतः किंचिच्छोधयन्तु विपश्चितः ॥२५४॥

प्रायश्चित्त-चूलिका ।

योगिभिर्योगगम्याय केवलायाविनाशिने ।
ज्ञानदर्शनरूपाय नमोऽस्तु परमात्मने ॥१॥
मूलोत्तरगुणेष्वीषद्विशेषव्यवहारतः ।
साधूपासकसंशुद्धिं वक्ष्ये संक्षिप्य तद्यथा ॥२॥
एकेन्द्रियादिजन्तूनां हृषीकगणनावधे ।
चतुरिन्द्रियकुन्थानां प्रत्येकं तनुसर्जनम् ॥३॥
उत्तरमूलसंस्थेष्वप्रमादाद्दर्पतश्छिदा ।
कायोत्सर्गोपवासाः स्युरिंद्रियप्राणसंख्यया ॥४॥
अथवा यत्न्ययत्नेषु हृषीकप्राणसंख्यया ।
कायोत्सर्गा भवन्तीह क्षमयां द्वादशादिभिः ॥५॥
षडत्रिंशन्मिश्रभावार्कमहैकेषु प्रतिक्रमः ।
एकद्वित्रिचतुःपंचहृषीकेषु सषष्ठभुक् ॥६॥
नित्यप्रमादः प्रमादी च प्रत्येकं सस्थिरोऽस्थिरः ।
मूलधार्युत्तराधारस्तस्यासंज्ञिविघातिनः ॥७॥
उपवासास्त्रयः षष्ठं षष्ठं मासो लघुः सकृत् ।
कल्याणं त्रिचतुर्याणि कल्याणां षष्ठकं क्रमात् ॥८॥
षष्ठं मासो लघुर्मूलं मूलच्छेदोऽसकृत्पुनः ।
उपवासास्त्रयः षष्ठं लघुमासोऽथ मासिकम् ॥९॥
एतत्सान्तरमाम्नातं संज्ञिनि स्यान्निरंतरम् ।
तीव्रमंदादिकान् भावानवगम्य प्रयोजयेत् ॥१०॥
साधूपासकबालस्त्रीधेनूनां घातने क्रमात् ।
यावद्द्वादशमासाः स्यात् षष्ठमर्धार्धहानियुक् ॥११॥
पाषंडिनां च तद्भक्तयोगीनां विघातने ।
आषण्मासं भवेत् षष्ठं तदर्धार्धं ततः परम् ॥१२॥

प्राणवधपत्रचिट्छुद्रचतुष्पदविघातिनः ।
एकान्तरष्टमासाः स्युः षष्ठाद्यन्ताश्च पूर्ववत् ॥१३॥
तृणमांसात्पतत्सर्पपरिसर्पजलौकसाम् ।
चतुर्दशनवाद्यन्तक्षमणानि वधे छिदा ॥१४॥
प्रत्यक्षे च परोक्षे च द्वयेऽपि च त्रिधानृते ।
कायोत्सर्गोपवासाः स्युः सकृदेकैकवर्धनात् ॥१५॥
असकृन्मासिकं साधोरसह्योषाभिक्षाषिणः ।
कषायादभियुक्तस्य परैर्वा द्विगुणादि तत् ॥१६॥
नीचः पैशून्यपुष्टस्य गच्छाद्देशाद्बहिष्कृतिः ।
तच्छ्रुत्वा मन्यमानोऽपि दोषपादांशमश्नुते ॥१७॥
सकृच्छून्ये समक्षं चानाभोगेऽदत्तसंग्रहे ।
कायोत्सर्गोपवासाः स्युः प्राग्वन्मूलगुणोऽसकृत् ॥१८॥
आचार्यस्योपधेरर्हा विनेयास्तान् विना पुनः ।
सधर्माणोऽथ गच्छश्च शेषसंघोऽपि च क्रमात् ॥१९॥
सर्वे स्वामिवितीर्णस्य योग्यो ज्ञानोपधेरपि ।
स्वामिना वा वितीर्यते यस्मै सोऽपि तमर्हति ॥२०॥
एवं विधिं समुल्लंघ्य यः प्रवर्तेत मूढधीः ।
बलवन्तं समासृत्य यो वादत्ते प्रदोषतः ॥२१॥
सर्वस्वहरणं तस्य षण्मासः क्षमणं भवेत् ।
योऽन्यथापि समादत्ते तस्य तन्मौनसंयुतम् ॥२२॥
क्रियात्रये कृते दृष्टे दुःस्वप्ने रजनीमुखे ।
सोपस्थानं चतुर्थं नियमाभुक्तिः प्रतिक्रमः ॥२३॥
नियमक्षमणे स्यातामुपवासप्रतिक्रमौ ।
रजन्या विरहे तु स्तः क्रमात् षष्ठप्रतिक्रमौ ॥२४॥
मद्यमांसमधुस्वप्ने मैथुने वा निषेवते ।
उपवासोऽस्य दातव्यः सोपस्थानश्च चेद्बहु ॥२५॥
तरुण्या तरुणः कुर्यात् कथालापं सकृद्यदि ।
उपवासोऽस्य दातव्योऽसकृत् षण्मासपश्चिमः ॥२६॥

स्त्रीजनेन कथाजापं गुरूनुल्लंघ्य कुर्वतः ।
स्यादेकादि प्रदातव्यं षष्ठं षण्मासपश्चिमम् ॥२७॥
स्त्रीजनेन कथाजापं गुरूनुल्लंघ्य कुर्वतः ।
त्याग एवास्य कर्तव्यो जिनशासनदूषिणः ॥२८॥
स्थातुकाम सः चेद्भूयस्तिष्ठेत् श्रमणमौनतः ।
आषण्मासमयः कालो गुरूद्दिष्टावधिर्भवेत् ॥२९॥
दृष्ट्वा योषामुखाद्यंगं यस्य कामः प्रकुप्यति ।
आलोचना तनूत्सर्गस्तस्य छेदो भवेदयम् ॥३०॥
स्त्रीगुह्यालोकिनो वृष्यरससंसेविनो भवेत् ।
रसानां हि परित्यागः स्वाध्यायोऽप्यविरोधिनः ॥३१॥
उपधेः स्थापनाल्लोभाद्दैन्याद्दानप्रकृतितः ।
संग्रहात् श्रमणं षष्ठमष्टमं मासमूलके ॥३२॥
रात्रौ ग्लानेन भुक्ते स्यादेकस्मिंश्च चतुर्विधे ।
उपवासः प्रदातव्यः षष्ठमेव यथाक्रमम् ॥३३॥
व्यायामगमनेऽमार्गे प्रासुकेऽप्रासुके मतेः ।
कायोत्सर्गोपवासौ स्तोऽपूर्णक्रोशे यथाक्रमम् ॥३४॥
धननीहारतापेषु क्रोशैर्वह्नि-स्वरग्रहैः ।
श्रमणं प्रासुके मार्गे द्विचतुःषड्भिरन्यथा ॥३५॥
दशमादष्टमाच्छुद्धो रात्रिगामी सजन्तुके ।
विजंतौ च त्रिभिः क्रोशैर्मार्गे प्रावृषि संयतः ॥३६॥
हिमे क्रोशचतुष्केऽप्यष्टमं षष्ठमीर्यते ।
ग्रीष्मे क्रोशेषु षट्सु स्यात् षष्ठमन्यत्र च क्षमा ॥३७॥
समतिक्रमणं मूलं लापंति श्रमणानि च ।
स्याल्लघुः प्रथमे पक्षे मध्येऽन्त्ये योगभंजने ॥३८॥
आजानुदघ्ने तनूत्सर्गः श्रमणं चतुरंगुले ।
द्विगुणा द्विगुणास्तस्मादुपवासाः स्युरंभसि ॥३९॥
दंडैः षोडशभिर्मेये भवन्त्येते जलेऽजसा ।
कायोत्सर्गोपवासास्तु जन्तुकीर्णे ततोऽधिकाः ॥४०॥

स्वपरार्थप्रयुक्तैश्च नावाद्यैस्तरणे सति ।
स्वल्पं वा बहु वा दद्यादज्ञातकालादिको गणी ॥४१॥
दण्डेण गणिना देयं जलयाने विशोधनम् ।
साधूनामपि चार्याणां जलकेलिमहासृणिः ॥४२॥
युग्यादिगमने शुद्धिं द्विगुणां पथि शुद्धितः ।
ज्ञात्वा नृजातं वाचार्यो दद्यात्तद्दोषघातिनीम् ॥४३॥
सप्तपादेषु निष्पिच्छः कायोत्सर्गाद्विशुद्ध्यति ।
गव्यूतिगमने शुद्धिमुपवासं समश्नुते ॥४४॥
भाषासमितिमुन्मुच्य मौनं कलहकारिणः ।
क्षमणं च गुरूद्दिष्टमपि षट्कर्मदेशिनः ॥४५॥
असंयमजनज्ञातं कलहं विदधाति यः ।
बहूपवाससंयुक्तं मौनं तस्य वितीर्यते ॥४६॥
कलहेन परीतापकारिणः मौनसंयुताः ।
उपवासा मुनेः पंच भवंति नृविशेषतः ॥४७॥
जनज्ञातस्य लोचश्च बहुभिः क्षमणैः सह ।
आषण्मासं जघन्येन गुरूद्दिष्टं प्रकर्षतः ॥४८॥
हस्तेन हंति पादेन दंडेनाथ प्रताडयेत् ।
एकाद्यनेकधा देयं क्षमणं नृविशेषतः ॥४९॥
यश्च प्रोत्साह्य हस्तेन कलहयेत् परस्परम् ।
असंभाष्योऽस्य षष्ठं स्यादाषण्मासं सुपापिनः ॥५०॥
क्रियापराधभाषायामप्यसंयतबोधने ।
नृत्यगाथेति चालापेऽप्यष्टमं दंडनं मतम् ॥५१॥
चतुर्वर्णापराधाभिभाषिणः स्यादवन्दनः ।
असंभाष्यश्च कर्तव्यः स गणं गणिकोऽपि च ॥५२॥
अज्ञानाद्व्याधितो दर्पात् सकृत्कंदाशनेऽसकृत् ।
कायोत्सर्गः क्षमा क्षान्तिः पंचकं मासमूलके ॥५३॥
कुड्याद्यालंब्य निष्ठूय चतुरंगुलसंस्थितिम् ।
त्यक्त्वोक्त्वा क्षमणं ग्लाने भुक्ते षष्ठं तथा परे ॥५४॥

काकादिकान्तरायेऽपि भग्ने क्षमणमुच्यते ।
गृहीतावग्रहे त्यागः सर्वं भुक्तवतः क्षमा ॥५५॥
महान्तरायसंभूतौ क्षमणेन प्रतिक्रमः ।
भुज्यमाने चले शल्ये षष्ठेनाष्टमतो मुखे ॥५६॥
आधाकर्मणि सव्याधेर्निर्व्याधेः सकृदन्यतः ।
उपवासोऽथ षष्ठं च मासिकं मूलमेव च ॥५७॥
स्वाध्यायसिद्धये साधुर्ग्रहेशादि सेवते ।
प्रायश्चित्तं तदा तस्य सर्वदैव प्रतिक्रमः ॥५८॥
एकं ग्रामं चरेद्भिक्षुर्गन्तुमन्यो न कल्पते ।
द्वितीयं चरतो ग्रामं सोपस्थानं भवेत्क्षमा ॥५९॥
स्वाध्यायरहिते काले ग्रामगोचरगामिनः ।
कायोत्सर्गोपवासौ हि यथाक्रममनूदितौ ॥६०॥
काष्ठादि चलयेत् स्थानात् क्षिपेद्वापि ततोऽन्यतः ।
कायोत्सर्गमवाप्नोति विचक्षुविषये क्षमा ॥६१॥
ऊर्ध्वं हरिततृणादीनामुच्चारादिविसर्जने ।
कायोत्सर्गो भवेल्लोके क्षमणं बहुशोऽपि च ॥६२॥
स्पर्शादीनामतीचारे निःप्रमादप्रमादिनाम् ।
कायोत्सर्गोपवासाः स्युरेकैकपरिवर्धिताः ॥६३॥
वंदनाविधमध्वंसे कालच्छेदे विशोषणाम् ।
स्वाध्यायस्य चतुष्केऽपि कायोत्सर्गो विकालतः ॥६४॥
प्रतिमासमुपोषः स्याच्चतुर्मास्यां पयोधयः ।
अष्टमासेष्वथाष्टौ च द्वादशाब्दे प्रकीर्तिताः ॥६५॥
पक्षे मासे कृतेः षष्ठं लंघने सप्रतिक्रमः ।
अन्यस्या द्विगुणं देयं प्रागुक्तं निर्जरार्थिनः ॥६६॥
चतुर्मासानथो वर्षं युगं लोचं विलङ्घयेत् ।
क्षमा षष्ठं च मासोऽपि ग्लानेऽन्यत्र निरन्तरः ॥६७॥
उपसर्गाद्रुजो हेतोर्दर्पेणाचेलभंजने ।
क्षमणं षष्ठमासौ स्तो मूलमेव ततः परम् ॥६८॥

दंतकाष्ठे गृहस्थार्हशय्यासंस्नानसेवने ।
कल्याणं सकृदाख्यातं पंचकल्याणमन्यथा ॥६९॥
अस्थित्यनेकसंभुक्तेऽदर्पे दर्पे सकृन्मुहुः ।
कल्याणं मासिकं छेदः क्रमान्मूलं प्रकाशतः ॥७०॥
समितीन्द्रियलोचेषु भूशयेऽदंतवर्षणे ।
कायोत्सर्गः सकृद्भूयः क्षमणं मूलमन्यतः ॥७१॥
द्रुमूलातोरणौ स्थास्नू आतापस्तद्द्वयात्मकः ।
चलयोगा भवंत्यन्ये योगाः सर्वेऽथवा स्थिराः ॥७२॥
भंजने स्थिरयोगानामपस्मारादिकारणात् ।
दिनमानोपवासाः स्युरन्येषामुपवासना ॥७३॥
तत्प्रतिष्ठा च कर्तव्याभ्रावकाशे पुनर्भवेत् ।
चतुर्विधं तपश्चापि पंचकल्याणमन्तिमम् ॥७४॥
सकृदप्रासुकासेवेऽसकृन्मोहादहंकृतेः ।
क्षमणं पंचकं मासः सोपस्थाने च मूलकम् ॥७५॥
ग्रामादीनामजानानो यः कुर्यादुपदेशनम् ।
जानन् धर्माय कल्याणं मासिकं मूलगः स्मये ॥७६॥
आलोचना तनूत्सर्गः पूजोद्देशेऽप्रबोधने ।
सोपस्थाना सकृद्देया क्षमा कल्याणकं मुहुः ॥७७॥
जानतस्यापि संशुद्धिः सकृच्चासकृदेव च ।
सोपस्थानं हि कल्याणं मासिकं मूलमावधे ॥७८॥
सल्लेखनेतरे ग्लाने सोपस्थाना विशोषणा ।
अनाभोगेऽथ साभोगे प्रभुक्ते मासिकं स्मृतम् ॥७९॥
स्यात्सम्यक्त्वव्रतभ्रष्टैर्विहारे मासिकं क्षमा ।
जिनादीनामवर्णादौ सोपस्थानांगसंस्कृतिः ॥८०॥
निमित्तादिकसेवायां सोपस्थानोपवासनम् ।
सूत्रार्थाविनयाद्येष्वंगोत्सर्गालोचने स्मृते ॥८१॥
सूत्रार्थदर्शने शैक्ष्येऽसमाधाने वितन्वतः ।
चतुर्थं निन्हवेऽप्येवमाचार्यस्यागमस्य च ॥८२॥

संस्तराशोधने देये कायोत्सर्गविशोषणे ।
शुद्धेऽशुद्धे क्षमा पंचाह्नोऽप्रमादप्रमादिनोः ॥८३॥
लोहोपकरणे नष्टे स्यात् क्षमांगुलमानतः ।
केचिद्धनांगुलैरूचुः कायोत्सर्गः परोपधौ ॥८४॥
रूपाभिघातने चित्तदूषणे तनुसर्जनम् ।
स्वाध्यायस्य क्रियाहानावेवमेव निरुच्यते ॥८५॥
योऽप्रियं करणं कुर्यादनुमोदेत चाथवा ।
दूरस्थोऽसौ जिनाज्ञायाः षष्ठं ·ापस्थितिं व्रजेत् ॥८६॥
तृणकाष्ठकवाटानामुद्घाटनविघट्टने ।
चातुर्मास्याश्चतुर्थं स्यात् सोपस्थानमवस्थितम् ॥८७॥
शश्वद्विशोधयेत् साधुः पक्षे पक्षे कमंडलुम् ।
तदशोधयतो देयं सोपस्थानोपवासनम् ॥८८॥
मुखं क्षालयतो भिक्षोरुदविंदुर्विशेन्मुखे ।
आलोचना तनूत्सर्गः सोपस्थानोपवासनम् ॥८९॥
आगंतुकाश्च वास्तव्या भिक्षाशय्यौषधादिभिः ।
अन्योन्यागमनाद्यैश्च प्रवर्तंते स्वशक्तितः ॥९०॥
विधिमेवमतिक्रम्य प्रमादाद्यः प्रवर्तते ।
तस्मात् संघादसौ वर्षमपनेयः प्रदुष्टधीः ॥९१॥
शिलोदरादिकं सूत्रमधीते प्रविलिख्य यः ।
चतुर्थालोचने तस्य प्रत्येकं दंडनं मतम् ॥९२॥
जातिवर्णकुलोनेषु भुंक्तेऽजानन् प्रमादतः ।
सोपस्थानं चतुर्थं स्यान्मासोऽनाभोगतो मुहुः ॥९३॥
जातिवर्णकुलोनेषु भुंजानोऽपि मुहुर्मुहुः ।
साभोगेन मुनिर्नूनं मूलभूमिं समश्नुते ॥९४॥
चतुर्विधमथाहारं देयं यः प्रतिषेधयेत् ।
प्रमादादुद्दुष्टभावाच्च क्षमोपस्थानमासिके ॥९५॥
ज्ञानोपकरणौषधं वाथ देयं यः प्रतिषेधयेत् ।
प्रमादेनापि मासः स्यात् साध्वावासमथो मुहुः ॥९६॥

चतुर्विधं कदाहारं तैलाम्लादि न वल्भते ।
आलोचना तनूत्सर्गं उपवासोऽस्य दंडनम् ॥९७॥
वैयावृत्यानुमोदेऽपि तद्‌द्रव्यस्थापनादिके ।
पथ्यस्यानयन सम्यक् सहाहादुपसंस्थितिः ॥९८॥
स्वच्छन्दशयनाहारः प्रमाद्यन् करणे व्रते ।
द्वयोरप्यविशुद्धित्वाद्धारणीयश्चिराग्रतः ॥९९॥
भूरिमृज्जलतः शौचं यो वा साधुः समाचरेत् ।
सोपस्थापनोपवासोऽस्य बस्तिवर्ण्यादिकेष्वपि ॥१००॥
चंडालसंकरे स्पृष्टे पृष्टे देहेऽपि मासिकम् ।
तदेव द्विगुणं भुक्ते सोपस्थानं निगद्यते ॥१०१॥
असंतं वाथ संतं वा छायाघातमवाप्नुयात् ।
यत्र देशे स मोक्तव्यः प्रायश्चित्तं भवेदपि ॥१०२॥
दोषानालोचितान् पापो यः साधुः संप्रकाशयेत् ।
मासिकं तस्य दातव्यं निश्चयोदंडदण्डनम् ॥१०३॥
स्वकं गच्छं विनिर्मुच्य परं गच्छमुपाददत् ।
अर्धेनासौ समाछेद्यः प्रव्रज्याया विशंसयम् ॥१०४॥
यः परेषां समादत्ते शिष्यं सम्यक्प्रतिष्ठितम् ।
मासिकं तस्य दातव्यं मार्गमूढस्य दण्डनम् ॥१०५॥
ब्राह्मणाः क्षत्रियाः वैश्या योग्याः सर्वज्ञदीक्षणे ।
कुलहीने न दीक्षाऽस्ति जिनेन्द्रोद्दिष्टशासने ॥१०६॥
न्यक्कुलानामचेलैकदीक्षादायी दिगम्बरः ।
जिनाज्ञाकोपनोऽनन्तसंसारः समुदाहृतः ॥१०७॥
दीक्षां नीचकुलं जानन् गौरवाच्छिष्यमोहतः ।
यो ददात्यथ गृह्णाति धर्मोद्दाहो द्वयोरपि ॥१०८॥
अजानाने न दोषोऽस्ति ज्ञाते सति विवर्जयेत् ।
आचार्योऽपि स मोक्तव्यः साधुवर्गैरतोऽन्यथा ॥१०९॥
शिष्ये तस्मिन् परित्यक्ते देयो मासोऽस्य दण्डनम् ।
चांडालाभोज्यकारूणां दीक्षणे द्विगुणं च तत् ॥११०॥

अनाभोगेन चेत्सूरिर्दोषमाप्नोति कुत्रचित् ।
अनाभोगेन तच्छेदो वैपरीत्याद्विपर्ययः ॥१११॥
क्षुल्लकानां च शेषाणां लिंगप्रभ्रंशने सति ।
तत्सकाशे पुनर्दीक्षा मूलात्पार्श्वंडिचेलिनाम् ॥११२॥
कुलीनक्षुल्लकेष्वेव सदा देयं महाव्रतम् ।
सल्लेखनोपरूढेषु गणेंद्रेण गणेच्छुना ॥११३॥
साधूनां यद्वदुद्दिष्टमेवमार्यागणस्य च ।
दिनस्थानत्रिकालोनं प्रायश्चित्तं समुच्यते ॥११४॥
समाचारसमुद्दिष्टविशेषभ्रंशने पुनः ।
स्थैर्यास्थैर्यप्रमादेषु दर्पतः सकृन्मुहुः ॥११५॥
कायोत्सर्गः क्षमा क्षांतिः पंचकं पंचकं क्रमात् ।
षष्ठं षष्ठं ततो मूलं देयं दक्षगणेशिना ॥११६॥
मृज्जलादिप्रमां ज्ञात्वा कुड्यादीनां प्रलेपने ।
कायोत्सर्गादिमूलान्तमार्याणां प्रवितीर्यते ॥११७॥
वस्त्रस्य क्षालने धाते विशोषस्तनुसर्जनम् ।
प्रासुकतोयेन पात्रस्य धावने प्रणिगद्यते ॥११८॥
वस्त्रयुग्मं सुबीभत्सलिंगप्रच्छादनाय च ।
आर्याणां संकल्पेन तृतीये मूलमिष्यते ॥११९॥
याचितायाचितं वस्त्रं भैक्ष्यं च न निषिद्ध्यते ।
दोषाकीर्णतयार्याणामप्रासुकविवर्जितम् ॥१२०॥
तरुणी तरुणेनामा शयनं गमनं स्थितिम् ।
विदधाति ध्रुवं तस्याः क्षमाणां त्रिंशदुदाहृता ॥१२१॥
तारुण्यं च पुनः स्त्रीणां षष्टिवर्षाण्यनूदितम् ।
तावन्तमपि ताः कालं रक्षणीयाः प्रयत्नतः ॥१२२॥
दर्पेण संयुतार्याथ विधत्ते दंतधावनम् ।
रसानां स्यात् परित्यागश्चतुर्मासानसंशयम् ॥१२३॥
अग्रहसंयुता क्षिप्रमापनेयापि देशतः ।
सा विशुद्धिर्बहिर्भूता कुलधर्मविनाशिका ॥१२४॥

तद्दोषभेदवादोऽपि पंडितानां न कल्पते ।
अन्योक्तं लक्षणीयं न तत्प्रहेयं प्रयत्नतः ॥१२५॥
यतिरूपेण वाच्यासा चेदार्यानामधारिका ।
हा ! हा ! कष्टं महापापं न श्रोतुमपि युज्यते ॥१२६॥
उभयोरपि नो नाम ग्राह्यं धिङ्नीचकर्मणोः ।
अन्यश्चेत्कोऽपि तद् ब्रूयात् पिधातव्ये ततः श्रुती ॥१२७॥
स नीचोऽप्यश्नुते शुद्धिं शुद्धबुद्धिः प्रयत्नतः ।
देशकालान्तरात्तत्र लोकभावमवेत्य च ॥१२८॥
शपथं कारयित्वाथ क्रियामपि विशेषतः ।
बहूनि क्षमणान्यस्य देयानि गणधारिणा ॥१२९॥
द्रव्यं चेद्धस्तगं किंचिद्बन्धुभ्यो विनिवेदयेत् ।
तदास्याः षष्ठमुद्दिष्टं सोपस्थानं विशोधनम् ॥१३०॥
येन केनापि तल्लब्धं पुनर्द्रव्यं च किंचन ।
वैयावृत्यं प्रकर्तव्यं भवेत्तेन प्रयत्नतः ॥१३१॥
भ्रातरं पितरं मुक्त्वा चान्येनापि सधर्मणा ।
स्थानगत्यादिकं कुर्यात् सधर्मा छेदभागपि ॥१३२॥
बहून् पक्षांश्च मासांश्च तस्या देया क्षमा भवेत् ।
बलं भावं वयो ज्ञात्वा तथा सापि समाचरेत् ॥१३३॥
क्षांत्या पुष्पं प्रवश्यंत्या तद्दिनात् स्याच्चतुर्दिनम् ।
आचाम्लं नीरसाहारः कर्तव्या चाथवा क्षमा ॥१३४॥
तदा तस्याः समुद्दिष्टा मौनेनावश्यकक्रिया ।
व्रतारोपः प्रकर्तव्यः पश्चाच्च गुरुसन्निधौ ॥१३५॥
स्नानं हि त्रिविधं प्रोक्तं तोयतो व्रतमंत्रतः ।
तोयेन स्याद् गृहस्थानां साधूनां व्रतमंत्रतः ॥१३६॥
श्रमणच्छेदनं यच्च श्रावकाणां तदेव हि ।
द्वयोरपि त्रयाणां च षण्णामर्धार्धहानितः ॥१३७॥
केचिदाहुर्विशेषेण त्रिष्वप्येतेषु शोधनम् ।
द्विभागोऽपि त्रिभागश्च चतुर्भागो यथाक्रमम् ॥१३८॥

षष्ठं स्याच्छ्रावकाणां तु पंचपातकसंनिधौ ।
महामहो जिनेन्द्राणां विशेषेण विशोधनम् ॥१३९॥
आदावंते च षष्ठं स्यात् क्षमणान्येकविंशतिः ।
प्रमादाद्गोवधे शुद्धिः कर्तव्या शल्यवर्जितैः ॥१४०॥
सौवीरं पानमाम्नातं पाणिपात्रे च पारणे ।
प्रत्याख्यानं समादाय कर्तव्यो नियमः पुनः ॥१४१॥
त्रिसंध्यं नियमस्यांते कुर्यात् प्राणशतत्रयम् ।
रात्रौ च प्रतिमां तिष्ठेन्निर्जितेंद्रियसंहतिः ॥१४२॥
द्विगुणं द्विगुणं तस्मात् शीलपुरुषे हतौ ।
सद्दृष्टिश्रावकर्षीणां द्विगुणं द्विगुणं ततः ॥१४३॥
कृत्वा पूजां जिनेन्द्राणां स्नपनं तेन च स्वयं ।
स्नात्वोपध्यंवराद्यं च दानं देयं चतुर्विधम् ॥१४४॥
सुवर्णाद्यपि दातव्यं तदिच्छूनां यथोचितम् ।
शिरः क्षौरं च कर्तव्यं लोकचित्तजिघृक्षया ॥१४५॥
क्षुद्रजन्तुवधे क्षांतिः षष्ठमन्यव्रतच्युतौ ।
गुणशिक्षाव्रतौ क्षान्तिरंगज्ञाने जिनपूजनम् ॥१४६॥
रेतोमूत्रपुरीषाणि मद्यमांसमधूनि च ।
अभक्ष्यं भक्षयेत् षष्ठं दर्पतश्चेद् द्विषट्क्षमा ॥१४७॥
पंचोदुंबरसेवायां प्रमादेन विशोषणम् ।
चांडालकारुकाणां षडन्नपाननिषेवणे ॥१४८॥
सद्योल्लंघि (चि) तगोघातबन्दीगृहसमागतान् ।
कृमिदष्टं च संस्पृश्य क्षमणानि षडश्नुते ॥१४९॥
सुतामातृभगिन्यादिचांडालीरभिगम्य च ।
अश्नुवीतोपवासानां द्वात्रिंशतमसंशयम् ॥१५०॥
कारूणां भाजने भुक्ते पीतेऽथ मलशोधनम् ।
विशोषा पंच निर्दिष्टा छेददक्षैर्गणाधिपैः ॥१५१॥
जलानलप्रवेशेन भृगुपाताच्छिशावपि ।
बालसंन्यासतः प्रेते सद्यः शौचं गृहिव्रते ॥१५२॥

ब्राह्मणक्षत्रविट्शूद्रा दिनैः शुद्ध्यंति पंचभिः ।
दशद्वादशभिः पक्षाद्यथासंख्यप्रयोगतः ॥१५३॥
कारिणो द्विविधा सिद्धा भोज्याभोज्यप्रभेदतः ।
भोज्येष्वेव प्रदातव्यं सर्वदा क्षुल्लकव्रतम् ॥१५४॥
क्षुल्लकेष्वेककं वस्त्रं नान्यन्न स्थितिभोजनम् ।
आतापनादियोगोऽपि तेषां शश्वन्निषिध्यते ॥१५५॥
क्षौरं कुर्याच्च लोचं वा पाणौ भुंक्तेऽथ भाजने ।
कौपीनमात्रतंत्रोऽसौ क्षुल्लकः परिकीर्तितः ॥१५६॥
सद्दृष्टिपुरुषाः शश्वद्धर्मोद्दाहाद्धि बिभ्यति ।
लोभमोहादिभिर्धर्मदूषणं चिंतयंति न ॥१५७॥
प्रायश्चितं न यत्रोक्तं भावकालक्रियादिकम् ।
गुरूद्दिष्टं विजानीयात् तत्प्रणालिकयानया ॥१५८॥
उपयोगाद्व्रतारोपात् पश्चात्तापात् प्रकाशनात् ।
पादांशार्धंतथा सर्वं पापं नश्येद्विरागतः ॥१५९॥
अवद्ययोगविरतिः परिणामो विनिश्चयात् ।
प्रायश्चित्तं समुद्दिष्टमेतत्तु व्यवहारतः ॥१६०॥
प्रायश्चित्तं प्रमादेऽदः प्रदातव्यं मुनीश्वरैः ।
अपि मूलं प्रकर्तव्यं बहुशो बहुशो भवेत् ॥१६१॥
गृहीतव्यं त्रयाणां न हितं स्वस्मै समीप्सुभिः ।
नरेन्द्रस्यापि वैद्यस्य गुरोर्हितविधायिनः ॥१६२॥
यावंतः स्युः परीणामास्तावंति छेदनान्यपि ।
प्रायश्चित्तं समर्थः को दातुं कर्तुमहो मते ॥१६३॥
प्रायश्चित्तमिदं सम्यग्युञ्जानाः पुरुषाः परम् ।
लभंते निर्मलां कीर्तिं सौख्यं स्वर्गापवर्गजम् ॥१६४॥
चूलिकासहितो लेशात् प्रायश्चित्तसमुच्चयः ।
नानाचार्यमतानैक्याद्वोद्धुकामेन वर्णितः ॥१६५॥
अज्ञानाद्यन्मया बद्धमागमस्य विरोधिकृत् ।
तत्सर्वमागमाभिज्ञाः शोधयंतु विमत्सराः ॥१६६॥

APPENDIX

The "Prāyaśchitta Grantha"

(1) For the use of any of the three *makāras* (flesh, wine, or honey)

12 fasts, 12 half-fasts, 50 *abhiṣekas*, 1 *kalaśābhiṣeka*, 24,000 flowers, 2 *tirthas*, 4 kinds of fruits, 1 cow, grain, sandalwood, and 3 *niṣkas* (Verse 2)

(2) For the above when committed in ignorance (V. 3)

50 *abhiṣekas*, 5,000 flowers, 2 *palas* sandalwood and 2 *tirthas*

(3) For the use of any of the *pancha* (five) *udambaras* (V. 4)

4 fasts, 12 half-fasts, 4,000 flowers, 2 *palas* sandalwood, 50 *bhojanas* and 1 *tirtha*.

(4) For dining at the places of *pariahs*, *malekshas* and the men of low-castes (V. 5)

30 fasts, 50 half-fasts, 200 *bhojanas*, 3 cows, 20 *abhiṣekas*, 5 *kalaśābhiṣekas*, 5 *amṛitābhiṣekas*, 100 *mukkulas*, *śrikhanda*, 20 palas sandalwood, 50,000 flowers, 5 *tirthas* and 20 *niṣkas*.

(5) For dining in the temples of *Bhils*, *Chamāras* and other such men (V. 6)

24 fasts, 50 half-fasts, 150 *bhojanas*, 2 cows, 3 *kalśābhiṣekas*, 15 *abhiṣekas*, 1 *panchāmṛitābhiṣeka*, 75 *mukkulas*, 15 *palas* sandalwood, 40,000 flowers, 10 *tirthas*, 15 *niṣkas*.

(6) For dining at the places of the men of the remaining 18 (low) castes (V. 7)

9 fasts, 30 half-fasts, 3 *kalaśābhiṣekas*, 3 *panchāmṛitābhiṣekas*, 25 *mukkulas*, 60 *bhojanas*, 3 cows, 10 *palas* sandalwood, 1,000 flowers, 2 *tirthas* and 5 *niṣkas*.

(7) For the death of a member of the family by fire and the like (V. 8)

25 fasts, 50 half-fasts, 200 *bhojanas*, 15 *abhiṣekas*, 3 *kalaśābhiṣekas*, 1 *panchāmṛitābhiṣeka*, 3 cows, 40,000 flowers, 75 *mukkulas*, 10 *palas* sandalwood, 5 *tirthas* and 15 *niṣkas*.

(8) For the death of a member of one's family by a fall from a horse, snake-bite, lightning-stroke or from an accident arising from purely material causation (V. 9)

5 fasts, 20 half-fasts, 25 *abhiṣekas*, 2 *kalaśābhiṣekas*, 10 *panchāmṛitābhiṣekas*, 25 *mukkulas*, 40 *bhojanas*, 2 cows, 10 *palas* sandalwood, 1,000 flowers, 5 *tirthas*, and 3 *niṣkas*.

(9) For causing the death of a *Brāhmaṇa* (V. 10)

30 fasts, 50 half-fasts, 2 *kalśābhiṣekas*, 10 *amṛitābhiṣekas*, 20 *mukkulas*, 2 cows, 100 *bhojanas*, 10,000 flowers, 10 *palas* sandalwood, 5 *tirthas* and 5 *niṣkas*.

(10) For dining with Jaina *Sudras* (V. 11)

30 half-fasts, 1 *kalaśābhiṣeka* 5 *panchāmṛitābhiṣekas* 12 *mukkulas*, 50,000 flowers, 2 *palas* *śrikhanda*, 1 *tirtha* and 2 *niṣkas*.

(11) For dining with non-Jaina *Sudras* (V. 12)

30 half-fasts, 3 *kalaśābhiṣekas*, 10 *panchāmṛitābhiṣekas*, 25 *mukkulas*, 1 cow, 10 fasts, 100,000 flowers, 5 *palas śrikhanda*, 100 *bhojanas*, 2 *tirthas*, and 5 *niṣkas*.

(12) For cohabiting with one's mother or daughter or with a woman of the *Chāndāla* (pariah) caste (V. 13)

50 fasts, 500 half-fasts, 3 *kalaśābhiṣekas*, 10 *panchāmṛitābhiṣekas*, 50 *mukkulas*, 2 cows, 200 *bhojanas*, 50,000 flowers, 15 *palas* sandalwood, 5 *tirthas* and 7 *niṣkas*.

(13) For living with the *kāru Sudras* (V. 14)

5 fasts, 10 half-fasts, 10 *abhiṣekas*, 10 *panchāmṛitābhiṣekas*, 20 *bhojanas* and 1,000 flowers.

(14) For dining at the places of *kāru Sudras* (V. 15)

8 fasts, 20 *abhiṣekas*, 5,000 flowers, 50 *bhojanas* and 2 *palas śrikhanda*.

(15) For impurity due to birth or death of a member in the family (V. 16)

(i) in the case of a *Kshatriya*	5 days' observance of non-participation in social rites (*sūtuka*)
(ii) in that of a *Brāhmaṇa*	10 days' ,,
(iii) in that of a *Vaiśya*	12 days' ,,
(iv) in that of a *Sudra*	15 days' ,,

together with 12 *abhiṣekas*, 6 fasts, and 3 *palas* of sandalwood.

(16) For the discovery of a piece of bone in the food in one's mouth (V. 17)

3 fasts, 6 half-fasts, 12 *abhiṣekas*, 60,000 flowers and 2 *palas* of sandalwood.

(17) Where the bone is discovered in the hand (V. 18)

2 fasts, 4 half-fasts, 8 *abhiṣekas*, 8 *bhojanas*, 4,000 flowers and 2 *palas śrikhanda*.

(18) For eating a thing that has been given up if it is not vomitted out (V. 19)

1 fast, 2 half-fasts, 4 *bhojanas*, 4 *abhiṣekas*, 3,000 flowers and 2 *palas śrikhanda*.

(19) For the uncleanness (impurity) consequent on the removal of a fœtus by means of operation or where the fœtus perishes in fire (V. 20)

12 fasts, 20 *abhiṣekas*, 5 *panchāmṛitābhiṣekas*, 50 *bhojanas*, 12,000 flowers, 1 cow, 5 *palas śrikhanda* and 3 *niṣkas*.

(20) For the destruction of herbivorous animal life (V. 21)

14 fasts, 25 half-fasts, 2 *kalaśābhiṣekas*, 22 *mukkulas*, 1 cow, 50 *bhojanas* and 12,000 flowers.

(21) For the destruction of a carnivorous animal through lack of vigilance (V. 22)

16 fasts, 20 half-fasts, 2 *kalaśābhiṣekas*, 5 *panchāmṛitābhiṣekas*, 40 *mukkulas*, 300 *bhojanas*, 1 cow, 300,000 flowers and 9 *palas* sandalwood.

(22) For the destruction, through lack of vigilance, of a bird (V. 23)

12 fasts, 1 *kalaśābhiṣeka*, 1 *panchāmṛitābhiṣeka*, 12 *mukkulas*, 11 *abhiṣekas*, 24 *bhojanas*, and 26 betel-leaves, 11 special forms of worship and 11 *kāyotsargas*.

(23) For the destruction of a creeping insect (V. 24)

11 fasts, 16 half-fasts, 16 *abhiṣekas*, 16 *Jina-pujas*, 60,000 flowers, 60 *bhojanas* and 60 betel-leaves.

(24) For the destruction of a water animal (V. 25)

11 fasts and 11 half-fasts.

(25) For the death of cattle whether in one's house or outside (V. 26)

11 fasts, 20 half-fasts, 1 *mahā-abhiṣeka* with 108 pitchersful of water, 20 *abhiṣekas*, 5 *panchāmṛitābhiṣekas*, 1 cow, 5 *bhojanas*, 50,000 flowers, 5 *palas* sandalwood and 5 *niṣkas*.

(26) Ditto if the dead animal happen to be a she-buffalo (V. 27)

23 fasts, 22 half-fasts, 8 *abhiṣekas*, 5 *panchāmṛitābhiṣekas*, 1 *kalaśābhiṣeka*, 30 *mukkulas*, 80 *bhojanas*, 20,300 flowers and 3 *palas* sandalwood.

(27) For the death of a man caused by the burning down of one's house (V. 28)

22 fasts, 22 half-fasts, 12 *kalaśābhiṣekas*, 5 *panchāmṛitābhiṣekas*, 20 *mukkulas*, 1 cow, 50 *bhojanas*, 20,000 flowers and 5 *palas* sandalwood.

(28) For the death of a child if it be crushed under one's body (V. 29)

15 fasts, 35 half-fasts, 35 *kalaśābhiṣekas*, 10 *panchāmṛitābhiṣekas*, 32 *abhiṣekas*, 8 *palas* sandalwood, 29,000 flowers, 1 cow and 5 *niṣkas*.

Explanation of Terms.

The significance of the special terms used in the appendix is as follows:

Half-fast means taking only one meal in twenty-four hours.

Abhiṣeka signifies bathing the Statue of the Tirthamkara (in the Temple) with water.

Kalaśābhiṣeka is the bathing of the Statue with a big pitcherful of water, ceremoniously.

Panchāmṛitābhiṣeka is the bathing of the Tirthamkara's Statue with milk, curd, sugar-cane juice, *ghee* (clarified butter) and the water of dried herbs.

Tirtha means worshipping at a Tirtha (place of pilgrimage).

Mukkula means a great worship ritual.

Niṣka=a measure of gold which may be 4 or 9 or 16 *mashas* (*i.e.*, 64, 144 or 256 grains) in weight.

Pala=4 *tolas*, that is, $1\frac{4}{5}$ ounces in weight.

Bhojana means feeding the number of men indicated

Cow, grain, *śrīkhaṇḍa, niṣka* and betel leaves are to be given as gifts to the deserving or to some one appointed in this behalf

Udambaras are the fruits of certain trees which contain milky juice or sap These are regarded as objectionable as a very large number of group-souls are found in them.

Śrīkhaṇḍa means a kind of pudding or sweetmeat.

Kāru Sudras are those members of the Sudra class at whose place men of the other three *varnas* can dine without objection

Jina-pūjā means the ritualistic worship of the Lord Arhant, which begins with *abhiṣeka* (bathing) and ends, usually, with *stuti* (adoration)

ERRATA

Page	line	from	for	read
52	17th	bottom	(12th and 20th)	(3rd and 4th)
69	4th	,,	vigilance[4]	vigilance[6]
75	1st	,,	191	193
,,	,,	,,	65	64
80	,,	,,	Ch. 68	Ś.68
87	5th	,,	*ratikramaṇa*	*pratikramaṇa*
90	2nd	,,	year[8]	year[3]
,,	1st	,,	add :[3] Ch. 65.	
93	11	,,	after 'one' add 'fast ;'	
,,	10th	,,	delete 'fast ;'	
96	1st	,,	add : [1]Ch. 72-74	
98	6th	top	delete 'carefully.'	
107	4th	,,	Guṇadharas	Gaṇadharas
117	,,	bottom	unwell[3]	unwell
120	3rd	top	create	to create
,,	19th	,,	saint	saints
124	4th	,,	milk	(milk
125	3rd	bottom	brother[6]	brother[7]
,,	1st	,,	add : [7] Ch. 132.	
126	,,	,,	add : [4] Ch. 193.	
130	7th	,,	period fixed	fixed period
165	6th	,,	*sūluka*	*sūtaka*